DR. LANCE A. CASAZZA

Be the Hammer Not the Nail

Because the Road to Success is Always Under Construction

The information contained in this book is intended to be educational and not for diagnosis, prescription, or treatment of any health disorder whatsoever. This book is sold with the understanding that neither the author nor publisher is engaged in rendering any legal, psychological, or accounting advice. The publisher and author disclaim personal liability, directly or indirectly, for advice of information presented within. Although the author and publisher have prepared this manuscript with utmost care and diligence and have made every effort to ensure the accuracy and completeness of the information contained within, we assume no responsibility for errors, inaccuracies, omissions, or inconsistencies.

Library of Congress Control Number: 2009941516

ISBN-13: 978-0-615-34154-5

Be the Hammer Not the Nail softcover edition 2010

Printed in the United States of America

For more information about special discounts for bulk purchases, please contact
3L Publishing at 916.300.8012 or log onto our website at www.3LPublishing.com.

Cover photo by Gail Shoop-Lamy

Book design by Erin Pace

This is dedicated to my mom,
the hammer that never gave up on this nail.

Table of Contents

Acknowledgements

To my Patients, you have taught me more than you'll ever know.

To my Friends, while we have celebrated many victories, you have displayed your truest character during defeat.

To my Team, Leslie, Kara, and all the others, for helping me build the practice of my dreams.

To Chiropractic, liberating me from SUBLUXATION, nerve interference and pain.

To Dr. Sidney B. Bean, the definition of TEAMMATE, the definition of FAMILY. I wish I could be half the MAN you already are.

To Dr. Charles Ward, you saved my life.

To my Siblings, for showing me chocolate is much sweeter with the nuts.

To Harry, my most valuable resource and my best friend. You should be my big brother.

To my Father, you have taught me how to help those that have nowhere to go.

To my Second Dad, thanks for believing in me.

To Mom, quite simply the most important person in my life, my ROCK, no acknowledgement will ever do you justice.

To Grandpa, you showed me it's not what you are, it's WHO you are.

To God, for gracing me with the tools I hope to share with others and being a better friend to me than I can ever be to you.

Introduction:
Hammers and Nails

Life is a do-it-yourself project. We are the foreman in charge of building whatever our life calls for. The main difference between people involves how they decide to approach the project. There are two types of people in the world — liberals and conservatives, boys and girls, believers and nonbelievers. This overly simplistic view can be used to explain almost any area of life. I see no difference when it comes to explaining how people approach life. Many believe that our path is already chosen, and that the decisions we make were set in motion a long time ago. Others believe in choice. They believe that you make your own destiny and choose your own path. They basically believe you make your own reality. Life can best be described as a game. You are playing that game right now, whether you like it or not. As with any game, rules and strategies apply to it. The better we understand the rules of the game and the best way to maneuver ourselves, the more likely we will prevail. So as you can see, the playing field has been predetermined and set in motion long ago, but how we choose to approach success is determined by what piece we choose to be while we play the game. There are two types of people in the world when building a life: hammers and nails.

Living and building your life as a hammer is an exciting one. That's what hammers do; they build things. They get to work on exciting projects, fix up trouble spots, and totally demolish things that need to be redone. Hammers also are very lucky — they constantly move around. Their job is never done. When a hammer builds one area, it will continue to the next challenge. Or sometimes it needs to repair an area that needs fixing to make it work again. It's in the hammer's nature to do this. It knows to define itself as a hammer requires the ability to build. Hammers are not perfect and do have some limitations. For starters, hammers only work when they have the proper plans and instructions on what to build. Also, a hammer cannot build something by itself; it must have other tools to help it complete the job. Notice that most hammers look alike, because they have common characteristics. They take charge of their lives and read motivational books, listen to positive CDs, attend seminars, and basically understand that the most important investment they make is the one between their ears.

Now nails on the other hand are exactly the opposite. For starters, with nails nothing is their fault. Everything that happens around them is because of circumstances out of their control or as the result of other people's actions. What do nails do in general? They sit in a bag waiting for something to happen. Even before that, they sat in a hardware store waiting for something to happen. And before that, they sat in a factory and eventually ended up in a hardware store waiting for something to happen. Most unhappy people do one of two things: They either hang out with other unhappy people or they suck the life out of everyone around them. Nails do similar things. They sit in a bag with other nails — people who think and believe the exact same way they do. Nails often curse at hammers for being "lucky," giving little credit for the hard work they put in. They laugh when a hammer misses its mark saying, "I told ya so," and even find joy when the hammer's project doesn't come out as planned. Nails that sit around too long get rusty — and these nails are very hard-to-repair, but it is possible to do so. The other useless nail is a bent nail; but once again, it can be straightened out with a little extra effort and willingness. The worst part: When the nail finally gets used, it gets stuck in one place and hardly moves at all. Oh, it has a part in the overall scheme of what is being built, but often feels like a victim. When a nail jams in place, a hammer most often pulls it out. Hammers will take these chance meetings to help the nail become a hammer. Sometimes the nail takes advantage of this new opportunity and sometimes not. What is for certain, the hammer will eventually stop helping and asking.

The truth is while there are a lot of people who are just straight hammers or nails, many of us will often waver between the two. Just as there are yo-yo dieters, good days and bad days, and times we feel in and out of control. Why do we sway back and forth? Being a hammer can be lonely because there are a lot more nails than hammers. In addition, being a hammer entails way more work. It requires getting up early, working multiple hours a day, and comes with an understanding that the day's work is never done. Being a nail is easy. It doesn't involve as much effort, and you have plenty of company as a nail. A nail serves a very important role and can enjoy a nice life being a nail. Things are nice and cozy when you're a nail, and when you get good and hammered into one place, you don't have to worry about dealing with change. Managing change is left to hammers that move from project to project. They understand that as they approach new challenges, what the plan calls to build will be different. The nail's plan calls for waiting around for something to happen, and when it does (or doesn't) to find something or someone to blame. Never realizing there are ways to become a hammer and that most hammers will help you and show you how. In fact, hammers ask nails all the time, but nails don't hear very well when they live in a bag with other nails — especially if it's a big bag and you're such a big nail you have sunk all the way to the bottom. Hammers as they continue to build become bigger and better hammers and advance to bigger projects, using more intricate plans. It's a classic case of the *rich getting richer*, which is funny because nails commonly use this mantra when discussing hammers. The more a nail is used, the more it gets used to being stuck in one place and cannot see that any other way exists, for nails truly believe that they could never be a hammer. They bought the other nails' lie that hammers are born and not made.

OK, this is all great! You've identified two types of people in the world, SO WHAT? Well, that's a very good question. A wise man once told me that in the introduction of any book you need to answer three basic questions: So what, who cares, and who the hell are you? Starting with so what, I believe the importance involves the identification of one group more prone to success while the other has a greater likelihood of failure. Let me be very clear: *You define what success means to you.* So by being open to this premise, we must deduce that the hammer group does something that fosters success while the nail group does something that hinders it. What I hear frequently from people and patients in my practice: They know what they should do, but for some reason they just don't do it. Therefore, we have identified two other things: Hammers and nails know what needs to be done, but for some reason hammers seem to be the only ones that do the building. Hence the million dollar, "So What?" is that to be successful, we just need to do what hammers do. The problem lies in the fact that if right now you are in the nail phase, you may not know how to get started. If you do know what needs to be done and you're not doing it, you need to implement a system to get you to start doing what the hammer types already are doing. This book lets you know what to do and puts it all together in a simple one-page system on how to do it.

Well, who cares? We all care. It is in our human nature and DNA to care. We do what we have to do to survive and adapt. It is in our nature to thrive and to grow, to never be satisfied. Why is this so important? There was a group that refused to adapt and gave up surviving and they are no longer with us. You may remember them, they are called dinosaurs. There are also modern day dinosaurs that refuse to adapt to a new way of thinking. I am happy to say that those kinds of attitudes are becoming extinct. How do I know that we care so much? We spend millions trying to find the answers and searching for the right drug or the amount of stuff we can accumulate to make us happy. We look for others to blame for the problems that surround us. We care what others think about us. We care that we might make a mistake or a wrong choice. We search for that almighty answer that will bring us happiness and success, which is basically why we do the things we do. Judging from the high rates of alcohol and drug use, it seems that many of us don't do a very good job. Scales that measure satisfaction of life are at the lowest they have been in history. Even with all of the technology and advances all around us to make our lives easier, things seem more difficult than ever. We have all of these devices such as faxes, email and PDAs created to free up our schedules for other things and yet we still seem to have less and less time. Why? We have been looking in the wrong place to find happiness. We have to refine our view of how we define success. We need to start shooting arrows at targets and not just all over the place hoping to hit something. We were born to build, but we were left with little instruction on how to do it.

Well OK! Who the hell are you Lance A. Casazza to tell me how to live my life? If you mean do I have formal training on the subject, I have none. I am not an expert. I did not go to school to become a coach, counselor or psychologist. I have never published a book (until now). Who I am is a person with dreams and challenges and similar to you, and I wasn't well equipped with how to approach them. From what I remember, life never came with an instruction book and if it did, I either lost it or never read it. To gain some perspective of where I was and how I got to where I am now, we need to take a trip back in time …

Chapter 1:
Late to the Party

"Life is not a journey to the grave with intentions of arriving safely in a pretty well-preserved body, but rather to skid in broadside, thoroughly used up, totally worn out and loudly proclaiming ... 'WOW! What a ride!'"
— Author Unknown

I started my life late to the party. As my due date came and went, it was decided that my mom should induce labor. This did not seem to work, introducing my first failure in life. So as a last-ditch effort to present me to the world and get my life underway, I was born by cesarean. This was pretty rare at the time and considered somewhat risky. Keep in mind the date was May 6, 1971. After a successful entrance, I was whisked away and considered a healthy baby. At this point, I decided to give my parents grief from the start. During this time period, babies were not kept with their parents. So when it came time to eat, I was taken to mom for feeding time. After two to three days of this ritual, it appeared that I made this pilgrimage without crying once. (Something that in this day and age would be considered a dream come true.) My mom consumed with having a "normal" baby, called our doctor upset that something was not right.

"Something is wrong," she exclaimed. "He doesn't ever cry."

My doctor, who I consider a very smart guy and maybe the first person who understood me, said, "Relax, relax, he is just a very happy and content baby."

"No, I know something is wrong," she replied.

"OK, the next time he comes to nurse, just hold him a few inches from the tap," said the doctor. She decided to do as he advised. When they brought me in, I lay anticipating the comfort I had become so accustomed to. My mom, doing as instructed, held me away from my target. "Whaaaaaaaaaaaaaaaaaaaaaaaa!" was my response. Thus, leading to one of my mom's oldest stories and jokes, "And he hasn't shut up since." In her defense, you would be hard pressed to find many who would disagree.

Barely a few days old, there would be many challenges to come. I was born with jaundice, as is the case with a large group of newborns. Then later they discovered that I had been born with a hernia. After doing whatever they do for an infant in this predicament, I was placed back with my team of newborns. However, they had run out of blue baby gowns. So doing what any sensible nurse would do, they placed me in a pink one. This was something that did not make Dad very happy — it was a little too much for a father in the early '70s. So there lay the boys in blue, the girls in pink, and me in a white concoction that the nurses had invented to keep my dad at bay. In a small way, I hope the experience helped me become in touch with my feminine side. Fathers can also get a little crazy with their firstborn — and my dad was no different. As if this wasn't enough, I was born pigeon-toed and was put in casts to correct the problem. Needless to say, I was born with "stuff."

In an effort to keep consistent with my early years, the journey through grade school was no different. My parents divorced prior to my entering the first grade. It was hard at the time and difficult to understand. It is also an excuse many use to justify failure — and it had little to do with my difficulty growing up. I feel certain about this because my parents constantly reminded me of how much they loved me, and the problems they were having had nothing to do with me or my sister. Without these early affirmations, the following years would have been much more difficult. School presented its own challenges. Not grasping reading and math like many of the other children, I was placed in the "special" math and reading group. This was a good thing because I was not up to speed with many of the other children. The bad part about it was that I identified early on that I was in the "slower" group. Let me concede educators have it tough in this respect. I needed to receive special attention to not be left behind. At an early age I believed that I wasn't that smart. More importantly, I programmed myself early that I could never be as smart as the other kids. For me, this situation became an early introduction of how to make excuses for failure.

I continued to crawl through grade school. I had many tutors, hours after school for extra help, and visits to therapists to find out what was wrong. The report was always the same, "He has the intelligence; he just isn't doing the work." Let me exclaim that no one was wrong. They were right. Looking back, I truly remember believing that I wasn't smart. So what was the point in trying? Maybe by avoiding doing the work left little risk for failure, but I never saw that there was also the possibility of success. *Early on in my life I programmed myself to only see losses, not celebrate wins.*

When I got accepted to Saint Francis High School in Mountain View, California, it was contingent upon my attending summer school prior to the beginning of freshman year. Another brain implant that I was not ready for my next level. I moved to live with my dad for high school and didn't know a soul. First day of high school, maybe one of the most tragic days of a teenager's life, and I knew no one. Somehow I was elected freshman class president, which to this day I believe I won because I had buttons that said, "Vote for Lance." High school was very hard for me. I had best friends in many different groups, jocks, rockers and scholars, but I was never fully in any group. I was never invited to a Sadie Hawkins dance and my prom dates were always from other schools.

I did find one love in high school and that was for the game of football. I enjoyed the hard work and camaraderie. I loved that there was a true definition of the amount of work you put in equaled the results you could achieve. I laugh because even knowing the equation I was still a pretty average player. At this time, I had yet another setback: I injured my lower back while training over the summer. It had gotten so bad that I collapsed at random times with no warning or reason.

After much therapy and treatment, the medical people suggested surgery for the perceived stenosis[1] that was causing my problem. I was told that I would never play football again but that I could walk and play golf. Well, I always expected to "walk," and I hated golf, so we began to look at other options. Little did I know how much this injury would affect my life. That is when I met Nick Athens, a chiropractor in town who had an excellent reputation for helping many people, including many professional athletes who swore by his care. Nick asked me to give him a few months to alleviate the nerve interference in my spine. To this day I have never collapsed again. Needless to say, I was intrigued by this form of care that could help me when others couldn't. Nick would tell me every time I came in, "You should do this. You'd be great at this." I truly believed he'd get money if I went to chiropractic school. The truth was he just loved what he did and wanted to share what he knew to help others. On the contrary, my father, who was a lawyer, came home every day and stopped in front of my door and said, "Lance, don't ever become a lawyer." I knew as early as age 15 that I wanted to be a chiropractor when I grew up.

My senior year I started on the football team. Looking back, it was the first time I felt accepted by the group and I did fairly well. However, the coach didn't think so and he made very little effort to hide it. He was also my high school guidance counselor. When schools called to recruit me, he either said I wasn't good enough or that my grades would never meet admission criteria. If I wanted to play in college, I was going to have to market myself. So I made my own tapes to send to schools (we had tapes in those days) and solicited schools I thought I could compete at.

While I had many schools in mind, I knew early that I wanted to attend University of California, Davis (UC Davis). It was a division two school at the time and one of the few that actually wrote me back. During this time, my coach/advisor encouraged me to look into the local junior colleges in the area. To be quite honest, he was probably right. For some reason I thought I could possibly get into Davis. My grades were average, but luckily my SAT scores shed some light on

[1] Stenosis: Spinal stenosis is a narrowing of one or more areas in your spine — most often in your upper or lower back. This narrowing can put pressure on your spinal cord or on the nerves that branch out from the compressed areas. (Source: Mayoclinic.com)

the fact that I was "smart enough." UC Davis admissions personnel surprisingly believed in me and encouraged me to apply.

When I went to the college advisory center I was sidetracked once again. Struggling to find a UC application, I asked my advisor (also my head coach) where to find them.

He asked, "Why?"

I replied, "I'm applying to UC Davis."

His response was (and I swear this is true), "Why? You'll never get in."

For some reason, maybe knowing they had an interest in me, I said, "I just figured I'd try anyway."

I applied and the wait was long. Most of my friends and classmates knew where they were going in the late fall. While many were sharing college destinations after graduation, I was hoping, praying and doubting where I would be the following year. During a discussion of college futures, a girl in my class mentioned she was going to Davis.

I said, "I'm waiting to hear from Davis, too."

She replied, "You'll never get into Davis if you haven't heard by now." And in looking back, this was January or February, much later in the acceptance process. Then, thank God, I was admitted. To be totally honest, to this day I'm not sure why. I was not a great football player and my grades were just good enough to get in. I like to think they felt my passion to attend their institution and that I came to them. To their credit, the majority of their success at that time was taking a chance on athletes most colleges deemed "not good enough." A chance I made good on, by playing for four years and earning my degree. One of the best parts was when the gal who said I would never get in found out.

"That's stupid you got in for *football*," she said.

I replied, "Who's stupid? You busted your tail and barely got in. I had fun and got in just like you!" I must admit my reply was immature — and I just said it to make her mad. But in reality, Davis was a division two school that didn't have the pull to get athletes they wanted in the back door. A note on her, she dropped out of Davis after one year.

Davis possessed its own challenges. For starters, I was a college freshman with braces on my teeth put on the summer before my senior year in high school, which are the worst two years I can think of to have them. I also don't think I was ready for college — too much freedom combined with so much responsibility. I took some early licks that made me doubt I even belonged there. For example, I received a D on my first college paper. I will never forget I put "mankind" in the paper and the teacher took off points, citing "sexist language."

I started to believe early on I was in over my head. I didn't know how to succeed in college. It may sound silly, but at the time I didn't know how. I spent more time hunting down people's notes and finding old papers. I should have just gone to the class, done the reading, and focused on my own work. It could have been the thought that I wasn't ready for college that actually held me back. It was probably also a bit of just being too lazy about going to class and doing the work.

The mere thought of grad school after college was being programmed out of my mind. At this time Palmer College of Chiropractic had an open house for prospective students. I took my former girlfriend and we went together. When the evening was over they gave us some materials and we headed home. As she looked over the course load, she exclaimed, "You can never pass these classes." Looking over them, I remember thinking she was right. School had always been a challenge, and I was going to sign up for four more years? Not to mention there were six to seven classes per quarter, many of which I would never have taken at the same time given the choice. I planted a seed early on that we all do too often, "I could never do that." Negative affirmations are like deliberately planting weeds in your brain. Like all good weeds, negative thoughts grow, and I started to look for other options of what career path I would choose.

Two days after my last college final I was given the opportunity to work overseas. The National Football League (NFL) had six teams that played in Europe under the name The World League of American Football. They gave me the title as assistant to the general manager (GM), and while I did report directly to the team's GM, I was really nothing more than a paid intern. It was one of the best experiences of my life. I lived in Glasgow, Scotland and worked in the city of Edinburgh. The team was named the Scottish Claymores, and they were just coming off a poor record the year prior.

My daily routine consisted of living with the team in Glasgow and seeing them off to practice each day. Then I would take the morning train into Edinburgh, quite often with the questions and needs conveyed to me from the coaching staff. While my main job was to assist the GM, I basically helped out and filled voids wherever necessary. One task (thankfully that was never discovered) involved taking thousands of dollars (pounds at the time) back with me to distribute to players and staff. I always found it funny people, who sat next to the "pot of gold" on the train, were unaware of it. The work was probably the best I had done for any employer at that time. In over 100 days during my stay I had three days off. It also rained 80 plus of those 100 days. My efforts did not go unnoticed. In fact, my boss had to send out a memo that they needed to pass it through him before they added any more tasks to my job description. Although I would never have asked him to do that, I was thankful he did.

Unfortunately, there was a small problem. I had become caught in the middle of a tale of two cities — the coaching staff and the office staff (i.e., labor vs. management). I would later learn this conflict is not too uncommon. In all fairness, the entire coaching staff was great and super supportive of my efforts; however, the head coach, not so much. While he often asked for my assistance with many tasks, sometimes they were not completed to his liking. "I ask you to do one thing, Casazza ..." It was always one thing. He never recognized the 800 other things *I slam dunked, nailed or hit out of the park!* In his defense, it was not his fault. I was management, also known as the enemy. I wasn't one of "his guys." I had also been told by many that he was incredibly loyal to his staff. I took two things home from that trip. The first, I realized that to get ahead in that kind of environment, you'd better be attached to a rising star — this was something I didn't want to bank my future on. I knew from that experience that I did not want my success determined by someone else's achievement. Second, we won the World Bowl when I was there — the first championship I had ever been a part of.

What Are You Going To Do With Your Life?

The months following my return from overseas were a fun time, but one of little growth. Guided by the idea of a paycheck and not a career, I bumbled around many jobs. I sold cars for a week. Sold life insurance for two months, and even loaded trucks for a while. They were all honorable jobs, just nothing that I was passionate about. Since the balance I was looking for was freedom and finances, I settled on a bartending job. It allowed me to go to the lake each day with my buddies and work at night. This went on for some time until my mom invited me down to San Francisco for lunch. I can't remember where we went, but I do remember the question she asked me: "What are you going to do?"

Not understanding the question, my reply was, "I'm bartending tonight and probably heading to the lake tomorrow."

"No," she exclaimed, "with your life!"

Needless to say, I didn't have an answer for her. To be truthful, I wasn't too sure myself. My life always seemed to have some kind of predetermined structure of where to be and what to do. I remember feeling at the time that I could be whatever I wanted to be, but what? To my mom's credit she made it very easy. "Figure out what you want to do and how I can help it become reality." She is a large reason for where I am today. So not being sure where to start and with the renewed feeling of deciding what to be now that I was "grown up," I went to talk with my college advisor back at UCD, Dr. Holly. I was an exercise science major at Davis and often the advisors there would have job opportunities come across their desks. I figured that would be as good a place to start as any. The advice I received was obviously a turning point.

Strolling up to the campus brought back some fond memories. I had set an appointment with Dr. Holly during his office hours. I couldn't really tell if he remembered me or not — and it really didn't matter. I was honestly only looking for job suggestions or offers, anything else would be a bonus. Walking down the hallway toward his office made me think of how easy we had it in college. As I entered his office, it was obvious by the look on his face that he had at least recognized me. We shook hands, sat down, and I watched him looking over my file. He then said something to me that changed my life. "Lance, I was looking at your file and I noticed that I allowed you to change your major to exercise science because you had planned on going to chiropractic school. What happened with that?" I had no answer.

What happened to my dream of being a chiropractor? The dream I had told people about ever since I was 15 — and the profession that saved my life and allowed me to attend this college and talk with this very advisor? What had gotten in the way of my dream? ME. I had let myself and everyone else talk me out of pursuing my dream. Then I started thinking, how did that happen? There are many things that led me to truly "forget" I wanted to do this. I called my mom and said, "I'm going to be a chiropractor."

The Baby Elephant at the Circus

So what is the point of strolling down memory lane? Allow me to share with you a story and give you some insight of the system in this book. *Tool 43, The baby elephant at the circus (a.k.a., Baby Elephant Syndrome).* Way back in the olden days, the circus would receive newborn elephants to incorporate into their show. The young elephants had no training and no experience and needed to be conditioned. Even at a very young age elephants are endowed with immense strength and ability to persevere through much adversity. In an effort to constrain this awesome power, trainers would chain these young ones down to keep them under control and teach them early what their boundaries and limitations were. By being chained down at such an early level of formation, the baby elephants were conditioned at a very young age about the boundaries that they could achieve and the limitations their environment provided.

Later as adults, these elephants began to accept the limitations that they had been conditioned to accept. Knowing this, the trainers no longer had to hold the adult elephants down by chains and simply used ropes to keep their disciples in line. Those who saw the elephants held at bay by a simple piece of rope were shocked. "Why doesn't that elephant try to run away?" "It could break that rope in a second if it wanted to." You know this and I know this, the problem is that the elephant does not. Due to conditioning, an animal with the potential to break through this simple restraint, perceives this barrier as real. We see the restraints on this animal as inconceivable because we know they can be broken, but the elephant has no clue of the potential and ability it was born to achieve. There's a little elephant in all of us.

We can learn some important lessons from our pasts. Our first lesson involves self beliefs conditioned in us over time. I hope the story of the baby elephant showed you that we are the ones who hold ourselves back the most. Many of our beliefs about ourselves are false but have been reaffirmed over time. Many of the barriers we believe exist have been constructed by us. An understanding that we programmed our own brains with false data empowers us to reprogram our belief system — and hence enables us to achieve desired outputs. Your mind is simply a computer and limited by the beliefs that have been stored up over time.

Another reason I thought it important to share my life's little stories is because we all have a story. We all bring a full glass to the table and when that glass is full, it can seem very difficult to put any more inside of it. I once heard a speaker named Bill Esteb at a conference. Pitchers of water sat on the tables. While he described things that had occurred in his life, he poured some more water in his glass. His glass was full before he had barely gotten through his high school years, and it continued to overflow as he added more and more that had occurred in his lifetime. At the end, he had a full glass and a lot of water on the floor. Then he poured the rest out. If your goal is to achieve success, you must come into any system or game plan with an open mind — an empty glass.

We all have "stuff," and I find it holds many of us back — that and the way we have conditioned ourselves over time. Understanding these two principles helps answer the question: "How in the world did I get here?" Just as you wish you could tell the elephant to simply break the rope, I am telling you the same thing. I can't make you do it, but if you accept these principles, it will help you take the next step to build the life you strive to attain. For now, think of these lessons as an enlightenment of invisible barriers we may have never realized existed. Unfortunately, breaking free from these barriers is not enough.

A Fresh Start

When I started Chiropractic College in the fall of '98, I was overcome with a sense of renewal — the feeling of being given a fresh start, one I had never felt before. Looking back now, even though I didn't know it at the time, I broke through the two conditions that I described earlier. The full glass I had coming in for some reason didn't seem as full. And isn't that what a fresh start does, empties a full glass? The other thing I decided was to be smart for once. Somehow, I made a conscious decision to break free from the chains I used as excuses for my shortcomings. Just like that I was going to simply do what I perceived the smartest students did: Go to class, take notes and study.

Graduate school was the first real taste of success I believe I had in my life. I wanted to succeed and be the best and by letting go of the past, I could become who I wanted to be in the future. It was funny how it worked out. I really started getting good grades and people thought I was smart. I tried to tell them that this was a new thing for me, but they didn't listen. People's perception of me started to change because my perception of myself had begun to change. Over the course of grad school I won every scholarship that existed at the time, became president of our student body, and eventually graduated valedictorian of my class. I even graduated with a perfect 4.0. It was only natural to believe that all the hard work I had put in would instantly translate into success. The toughest part was now behind me. I thought I had arrived and by doing so, there was little work left to be done. I was going to build my practice and begin to reap some rewards from the years of sacrifice and effort I put in.

Reality Sets In

The early years of my practice were filled with many highs and lows. I was overwhelmed with the challenges that were presented to me as I opened my doors. So many things happened that I didn't expect and many more aspects that I didn't know how to handle. The problems of my practice were becoming unbearable, and I was starting to have self-doubt. How could this be happening to me? I was the smartest guy in school. I won all the awards and everyone told me how great I would do in private practice. I was supposed to be a "sure thing" and instead I was on the verge of failure. All the old feelings from before came back. I started having doubts about myself — and questioning if I could make it as a chiropractor. I kept asking, "What was wrong? Why was I failing?"

In chiropractic school I had been given instructions and tools of how to succeed — INSTRUCTIONS and TOOLS. There were also teachers who acted as coaches and goals that were focused on where to go and what needed to be done by what date. I realized that I needed help. It was in my search for that help that I discovered all that I am about to share with you in this book. It is all that knowledge that accumulated from that search that I will be passing on to you. It's so simple and, it is stuff that you probably already know. Then why this book you ask? Because what I learned can only help if applied. I believe it is not applied because many find it too hard or too much work or they don't have enough time. Would you give a program a shot that only had one page that you were required to review every 21 days? If your answer is "yes," then continue to read on. If your answer is "no," then continue what you are doing and expect the same results.

Live Your Dreams

I want to emphasize that the road to success is always under construction. That is what I forgot on my journey — and many don't even know. You are never going to arrive; there is no "Ta da I made it." You have to constantly work at life and to make a dream happen. I'll let you know another thing — you never reach a dream. To reach a dream means you have reached a destination, which means stopping. You don't reach a dream, *you live a dream.* This was one of my preconceived notions. I thought I had reached my dream. Not true, I had just begun to live my dream, and if I was going to continue to live it, I had to work on it. I still have work to do — and in developing this book I had the opportunity to focus on the process, learn more, and pass it on. I felt compelled to take all that I was learning to develop a system so others could benefit.

What most people don't realize is plans exist on how to build everything around us. Some call them blueprints, others call them instructions; but one thing is for sure, they exist for things that are built. Buildings, cars and cabinets all have instructions on how to be constructed. My path of self-discovery made me come to wonder, why do we have instructions for all these simple things to build but don't have instructions for the most important thing to us, our life? As I mentioned before, if I was born with a handbook, I lost it a long time ago or never read it. I'm sure that's a surprise knowing my early scholastic history. So I did what any normal person would do. I searched for some keys to life. I tried to read and listen and discover the things that people were doing that were successful. As I found these things, I discovered them to be true. They were all around us and they worked when applied. Then what was the shortfall? Why weren't they working for some people?

Well, I found some things out. The first was that many people don't know about the secrets of successful people. I know I didn't. The second was that many of the books and systems out there just had too many tapes and CDs and forms to fill out. Basically it all seemed like homework and for someone overwhelmed with everyday life, it just seemed like too much to handle. And last and maybe the most important, when trying to build what the plan calls for, you can't build without *Tools*.

They say the opening chapter of any book is a promise to the reader. Here is my promise to you. I am going to present to you a one-page blueprint of proven strategies to improve your life. I am going to give you instructions on how to fill out that one-page blueprint. Then finally, I am going to give you a set of *Tools* to help you build what your plan calls for. That's it. I have made it as easy as I can: One page to focus your efforts to have a successful life defined by what success means to you. If you are not willing to do one page, then there is no drug, secret or surgery that will bring you happiness. You will always continue to be a nail. But if you want to build like a hammer, I have the blueprint, I have the instructions, and I have the *Tools*.

"Most people will spend more time planning a vacation than planning their own life."

A common buzz phrase I hear a lot these days is "my carbon footprint," meaning the goal is to leave as little as possible. With regard to this book, what footprint will you leave? What impression will you have made? What will they say about you when you die? Maybe just as big a question of what awaits us on the other side is what will I leave on this side? We define this as our legacy. To leave a legacy you have to build a legacy — that's what this book is all about, building. You need to constantly build, and you need to be a hammer to build. *Tool 53* states, *"For those who believe, no proof is needed and for those who don't, no proof is enough."* This book will help you achieve success if you are willing to empty your glass and un-chain the past. Now grab your hammer and let's get to work.

Chapter 2:
The Blueprint

"Cherish your visions and your dreams as they are the children of your soul; the blueprints of your ultimate achievements."
— Napoleon Hill

I would like you to hold up your goals right now. Go ahead, just hold them up. You can go get them if you need to, I'll wait. The truth is most of you reading this book do not have your goals written down. The small group of you that have goals written down may have trouble reaching them. I discovered goals are not enough. Goals provide a target or roadmap for where you want to go in your life — a structure if you will. But if you don't have the proper *Tools*, it becomes more difficult to build what the plan calls for — the life of your dreams.

I have always found that I learn better when the message is explained in the form of an analogy. I think the best way to understand the system set forth in this book is to think about your life as a house. Houses are similar in many ways and also unique in different ways, just like people. Some houses are well-kept while others need a lot of work. Some houses expand and improve, while some houses fall into disrepair. What does your house say? Not to worry, *Be the Hammer Not the Nail* is basically about turning *you* into a handyman for your own life to maintain, repair and sometimes remodel troubled areas. You will learn how to write the plans, read the plans, and then most importantly, discover the *Tools* that make the plans become reality.

In this chapter, you will uncover all the important parts of the blueprint. These parts consist of the Mission Statement, Timeframe, Future Pacing, Goals + Affirmations, *Tools,* and Your Sign of Commitment. Seems like a lot, but a lot goes into building a house. The "foundation, framework, plumbing, electrical" offer a few examples. When many of the parts are in place, a house luckily starts to transform into a *home*. It resembles what you want your life to look like. Keep in mind that YOU determine what success means to you. As with learning any new skill it will at first seem awkward and different. You may even find yourself lost at times. Trust me, it will come together and with practice it will become automatic.

Some people describe their lives as "organized chaos." Many others are just plain unhappy. Why? Because what I am about to show you is not taught in schools. In addition, many resources exist for goal setting, but goals only give you direction toward where you want to be; they don't take you there. Success requires action, which translates into "building." As you will soon discover — and what makes this book unique, is having a set of awesome *Tools* to help transform goals into success. As you continue through the rest of this chapter, please read and try to learn the different aspects of the *Be the Hammer* blueprint. **Please do not attempt to fill in your blueprint now.** If you like, take time between sections to reflect or take notes on what you've just read and how it might apply to you. We will begin sketching our blueprints in Chapter 3 when I provide you with instructions.

What's Your Mission?

What are you all about? I know this is a weird question, but do you even know? What statement would best describe who you are? Who you want to be? In one paragraph, how would you describe where you want your life to be and how you hope others perceive it? Chances are it won't completely match the person that you are right now. I often find it totally contradicts what your life displays. The mission statement creates the foundation for your life (a.k.a., your "house").

Mission Statement

_____

_____

_____

_____

_____

_____

_____

Without it, neither can exist. You can have a great "yard," nice "paint job," great looking "windows" or "doors." Maybe even the best furniture money can buy; however, when that foundation is shaky, no matter how things appear on the outside, your house is a precarious mess; and when the foundation is really shoddy, your house is at risk of collapse at anytime.

Next you should be aware of the value and importance of a mission statement for your life, but most people associate a mission statement with business. For any company to be successful, they must have a written mission statement, which defines the company's identity and what they do or create. Most companies stay on track and keep their word because its people write down this information in a statement. More importantly, most companies will put it on display in the lobby. Businesses disclose their mission statements to new employees and potential investors. By doing so, it holds them accountable and provides little opportunity to stray off course. Their vision statement comes later (a.k.a., the goals of the company) or where they plan to go. We will get into this part later in the chapter.

In the meantime, here is your opportunity to define yourself. The best part of my system allows you to be the person you desire and have the life you want to enjoy — all because you DEFINED it. When you write down who you are and what you are about, you will likely achieve goals and avoid pitfalls. Please note: Your first personal mission statement may be difficult to write and possibly will have some changes later as you personally develop your new life. So let's look at some ways to get started.

The simplest way I can describe what a personal mission statement includes involves answering and describing who, what, when, where and why about you. Who are you? What are you going to do to be that person? When are you going to apply this action? Where can you apply this statement? Why are these things important? Please be aware, there is no right or wrong answer for your mission statement. It can be as long as a page or as short as a sentence. I have provided a paragraph-size space for you to write your response. I believe this space is big enough to give room to write a solid statement with regard to what your life is all about.

I recently stumbled upon my very first mission statement. So here is a good example of what it might look like:

I will do all in my power to give the best to my patients.

I will be the best son, brother, godfather, nephew I can be.

I will treat my body more like a temple and work to be in optimal shape.

I will make writing my goals, reading my goals, and refining my goals a daily ritual.

I will be a good friend and try to understand my friends are not me, and I will try not to put my expectations on them.

I will listen. Period.

I will try better to recommit myself to God.

I believe I can have a meaningful and long lasting relationship if I focus on what I am looking for.

I accept that I am human and that I make mistakes, but will use these as learning experiences to help me grow.

I like to think my present-day statement is different and has evolved from my first attempt. Yours will change as well. You may struggle to put anything on paper your first try. This roadblock is very common and to be expected. Just remind yourself you're trying — that effort in and of itself is a large symbolic gesture that you want to grab control of your life, who you are, and where you want to be. Keep in mind many ways exist to write your statement. When you read Chapter 3, which provides instructions on writing your blueprint, I give you some exercises to help you write your first mission statement. You will also learn a little about yourself from creating one. Begin to think about what you want your mission statement to say. What's the "foundation" for your life going to look like? Then keep reading to discover the next section of the blueprint.

You Need a Timeframe

When you do work on a house, it needs to have a timeframe. When you have a contractor or handyman come over to do work on your house, you expect him or her to tell you when the work will be done. If you expect that for work being performed on your home, why don't you have the same expectations for work on your life? The next part of the blueprint incorporates the aspect of time. Time is an important component of building a successful life. We hold ourselves back by saying, "Someday I will [fill in the blank]." *Tool 35, The road named someday leads to the town of nowhere.* Assigning a timeframe to goals, dreams and desires greatly increases the probability of success. When we implement a timeframe, it also forces us to constantly reevaluate and refine our goals. Let's look at how we use time in our blueprint.

When many people try to build the life of their dreams, the daunting task of changing bad habits holds them back. Bad habits hinder growth. Developing plans to achieve success become stalled because changing these habits seems too hard to do. The results cause bad to become worse, and the ability to begin a plan or achieve a plan becomes more difficult. I have good news, breaking a bad habit is not as hard as it seems. It has become commonly accepted that it takes 21 days to change any habit. Only 21! That's just three weeks or 75 percent of a month. When we look at changing habits in this timeframe, I don't think they look as scary anymore. You have heard hundreds of times that a journey of 1,000 miles starts with one single step. To put this into better perspective, I once heard a coach say, "A mountain climber falls when he only focuses on the top."

In addition, within 21 days, the first day is the toughest — and then in the days that follow the process often becomes easier. The good news: Every day becomes easier than the last one. Doesn't that sound like something to look forward to?

On the flip side, habits are not always a bad thing. There may be some good habits we try to start or reinforce. The 21 days goes for those "good habits" as well. For example, if you try to get up earlier, doing it for 21 days drastically increases your chance of success. If you didn't know this, you may try for three or four days, maybe even a week, but most likely you quit because it wasn't working for you. It didn't work until now, *because you didn't know how long to give yourself!* More good news: The power of 21 works for more than just habits.

I also want to share something everyone in the goal-setting community already knows: Goals need times and dates. To accomplish a goal it requires a time of completion. This is goal-setting 101, kindergarten for goal setters, or my favorite, goal setting for dummies. Listen to the following two statements: "My goal is to read one book a week." "My goal is to be reading one book a week by the end of the next 21 days, May 31st." Do you see the difference? Saying that you want to do something with an open-ended deadline means it could happen in the next month, year or never. By definition, a goal without a deadline or an assigned timeframe is not a goal at all. I can promise that if you don't attach times to goals, they almost never happen. When you approach goals as the second sentence description, you hold yourself accountable. You can recommit to unaccomplished goals or reassess, reevaluate and recalculate how better to make them a reality.

This initiative leads us to the final step in using a timeframe in setting our goals and in building a successful blueprint for life — the last part of the 21-day timeframe might be the most important and the most underutilized in goal setting and personal improvement. It involves the necessity of reviewing and rewriting your plan. I developed this part of the plan because of struggles I had with reaching my own goals. I would write them down and then they sat stuck on the fridge or office corkboard, and I occasionally looked at them. Just having them written down did honestly work now and then. I would look at them and say, "Hey, I just did that last week," but for the most part I was inconsistent. Consistency is key. The best teams and athletes thrive on repetition and doing it over and over and over until it becomes automatic. With the system I am providing, you will rewrite the entire blueprint every 21 days. Some things will change while oth-

Mission Statement

_____

_____

_____

_____

_____

_____

1 2 3 4 5 6 7 8 9 10 11 12 13 14 15 16 17 18 19 20 21

ers will remain the same — and while you will be reading the worksheet every morning and every night, you will reinforce this template for your life by periodically (every 21 days) rewriting it.

You will enjoy many benefits of rewriting the worksheet too. For starters, my dad once told me something I never believed at the time, but now understand to be true. He said, "When you write something and then rewrite it, it goes up your arm and into your brain." Now we all know there is no direct connection from arm to brain per se, but he described a method of reinforcement. Reinforcing our goals, desires and dreams enhances the probability of success. Second, it forces you to stay on top of all the parts of the plan.

You might decide to remove goals that have now become routines or habits. You may modify goals that have not been met. You will also add new goals that you now wish to achieve. In the sections to come I will expose you to how to divide these goals into long- and short-term. In addition, the short-term goal section will be divided into four areas. For now, accept the power of 21. Begin to contemplate habits that you wish to instill and ones you hope to shed. You can take comfort that ways exist to make these a reality. Also, celebrate that by revisiting your blueprint every 21 days, you will be able to stay on top of your plan for success. You will marvel at the "wins" you achieved and tinker with the areas of difficulty. By using time to your advantage, you lessen the possibility of it slipping through your hands.

Rome Wasn't Built in a Day

When you build a home, you will find things that need to be immediately done — walls, plumbing, electrical and roofing. Then there are some things you want to do but are not required to do right away — pool, satellite system or workout room. We want those things to complete the home, but we don't need them right this second. What I really mean is we need to pace ourselves or "future pacing."

What do I mean exactly by future pacing? Future pacing applies a strategy used by your blueprint sheet that keeps long-term goals on the table without an exact timeframe for completion. In the section of the plan right after the numbers one through 21, you will find a set of Roman numerals (get it? Rome wasn't built in a day). Use the six areas to place dreams that you would like to accomplish down the road (a.k.a., "future pacing").

Keep in mind, these long-term goals will differ from short-term goals. Short-term goals will come in the next section and adhere to our 21-day timeframe. These Roman numerals are slots for things that you want to keep fresh in your mind, but are not as time sensitive as the short-term goals that require action now. For example, I added my dream to one day speak another language. It does not have to be done today — and I can even live if it doesn't happen. I do want to constantly remind myself of my dream — and I can accomplish it when I'm ready or I can change it to a short-term goal — and hopefully one day a reality.

I'll give you some neat examples of how this works. When I started entering my desire to someday learn another language on my blueprint, things happened. First, it seemed like every other commercial on TV was for a CD system on how to learn another language. Then on top of that, while walking through the mall, one day I spotted a kiosk with another system on how to learn foreign languages. I finally started to feel really strange when one of my best friends asked me if I wanted to take an Italian class with him. I looked around and at the "universe" and said, "I got it." Now in all honesty these could have just been a string of coincidences and I can live with that; however by future pacing, these coincidences become more common and more evident. I do believe that because I had them written down on my blue-

Mission Statement

_____

_____

_____

_____

_____

_____

1 2 3 4 5 6 7 8 9 10 11 12 13 14 15 16 17 18 19 20 21

I.   **II.**   **III.**

IV.   **V.**   **VI.**

print that I read daily and rewrote every 21 days, I was more apt to see these little hints all around me.

Another common example for goal-setting involves weight issues. The majority of us have a target weight we would like to achieve. Put your target weight here _____. Most people are pretty far away from that weight. You'll find the Roman numeral section of the blueprint provides the perfect place to state your target weight. For example, let's say right now you weigh 240 pounds and your target weight is 200. You would enter 200 pounds into the Roman numeral section. Then coming up in the next section of the blueprint you enter short-term goals — and as you will discover, you will take your first step toward accomplishing your target weight. It will look something like, "Get to 235 pounds in X number of weeks." If you simply focus on your target weight, it seems unattainable. It's like taking a steak and cutting it into pieces versus trying to shove the whole thing in your mouth. Once you have bite-sized pieces, you can start to eat it without choking on it. What is the take-home message? _Separate long- from short-term goals and you are much more likely to achieve both._

We mentioned earlier that your mission statement was like the foundation, which provides the "base" for building your structure. We now need to know what we're building; this relates to the vision statement that we formerly alluded to. It provides direction and short-term goals for what we want to build — and we need a solid structure for what we are trying to build. The next section of your blueprint focuses on the "framework" for the life you want and the structure required for its success.

Goals + Affirmation = SANE

Within any blueprint there is a framework that needs to be built. It is the ultimate design of this framework that transforms concept into reality. Constructing the life of your dreams is no different. With the proper structure and framework built, the likelihood of designing the life you hope for has a much greater chance of success. To do this, you need to know how to build the frame. You need to know the frame's parts and responsibilities. In addition, when the framework needs to be tweaked, repaired or completely remodeled, you need to know where and how to do this. If you were to build a house and had little knowledge about the framework, many would call you insane and would have safety concerns about your house. This section introduces you to the parts of the framework and gets you in what I call Self, Affirmation, Nutrition and Exercise (SANE). I believe that when you focus on these areas and with clear direction, you tremendously increase your probability for success. These areas of short-term goal setting create the structure of life.

When you use these areas to create and aim for targets — and you work and rework them — you head in a positive direction — and your life becomes congruent. When just one of these areas turns into a mess, it makes personal growth a chore. For example, if a perfect home has a plumbing problem it doesn't matter if the rest of the house has great structure; it would become messy and unlivable. In the pages that follow, I will explain in detail all four parts to the SANE system and how you can tweak, repair or build the life you want.

Mission Statement

_____

_____

_____

_____

_____

_____

_____

1 2 3 4 5 6 7 8 9 10 11 12 13 14 15 16 17 18 19 20 21

I.   II.   III.

IV.   V.   VI.

Self:

Affirmation:

"

"

Nutrition:

Exercise:

Self

The first part of the blueprint's SANE section is Self. Self pertains to all the things you hope to accomplish in the next 21 days that have only to do with you. Leaving out Nutrition and Exercise, what goals do you hope to accomplish over the next three weeks? It might be to get up earlier, read one book a week, or become involved in a local charity. Some may say this sounds like a to-do list, but it's not. To-do lists are tasks — things that we do that need to be done on a daily basis but that don't improve personal growth. Remember, we are trying to instill goals that we want to achieve with the plan of eventually reaching them or making them habits. We will get into managing this section in Chapter 3 when I give you instructions on how to use and manage your blueprint.

To give you just a glimpse of what to expect, this section will sometimes change, modify or remain the same. When we review our blueprint every 21 days, we will analyze our status in regard to what we wrote down. If your goal was to get involved in a local charity and you are now doing that, you may revise that goal to hold a position in that charity. Are you starting to see how the progression of growth will begin to occur? Another key point to these sections is to make them doable. The space of entry is limited for a reason. I would say enter three to five things per three-week period. This will ensure that you hit a few of your targets. You may not hit all or any every time; that's why we review and refine.

Another thing to keep in mind is there may be something entered in a section that you choose to keep on there as a permanent reminder. If your goal is to get up earlier, and you have been regularly accomplishing that goal, but fear that this is an area of possible weakness, keep it on there at every revision. I do this for a few things. What is great about this is that you have identified an area of personal importance — and to emphasize that importance, you want a constant reminder. Winners possess this quality — the ability to identify trouble areas and use any means to avoid these pitfalls. Successful people embrace this quality on a daily basis.

Finally, if you missed one of your goals, rewrite it on your next blueprint. When doing so, try to identify why your goal was not achieved. Was it too unrealistic?

Is it no longer a goal? Also, don't dwell on it; chances are you hit other marks you were aiming to achieve. In addition, the growth process also includes the ability to identify trouble areas. We celebrate our wins and our losses. Why? Because the wins are what we strive for and the losses teach us how to be better winners.

Yet goals are not enough to help build a structure. Building a structure for a better life calls for a mantra. It requires that the workers (you) who construct the project have a motto that they use every day during the building process — this is commonly known as an affirmation and is the next part in the SANE system.

Affirmation

Tool 23, If I talked to you the way you talk to yourself, you'd hate me. Think about the things we often say to ourselves. "I'm an idiot." "I'm fat." I'm this … I'm that." We are sometimes serious and other times we are just kind of kidding with ourselves. The subconscious mind regardless of what our internal dialogue suggests can't tell the difference — and when we do it over and over again, our brain starts to believe and act on it. I believe our negative internal talk comes from societal conditioning. If you say, "I'm a great person." I'm hot." "I'm the best" "I love me," you are considered conceited or stuck on yourself. Obviously we don't like to be considered "conceited," so we don't say these things to ourselves or outwardly to others.

I am here to tell you that not saying these positive things to yourself is, in my opinion, one of the top five reasons why people fail to reach goals and find happiness in their lives. The key to personal growth calls for positive self-talk and can be done in the form of an affirmation. Affirmation means positive assertion. You can use your affirmation as part of your self-growth process or blueprint by writing down and speaking to yourself mentally and out loud.

Now I admit that when I first learned of the concept of affirmation and positive self-talk, I thought it was for weak people. I believed that people who did this were weird and just kidding themselves. Well, I was totally wrong and it turned out the joke was on me. You see the majority of successful people use affirmations as a tool for success. Many will go right ahead and tell you so. The ones that deny using them are either telling a little fib or may not even realize they are doing so. They may even talk to themselves in the mirror every morning and not even realize this act becomes a large part of how our brains implement affirmations every day.

Now you may wonder how affirmations got such a bad rap. Well, as I just mentioned, you can use affirmations by talking to yourself in a mirror. It is a well-accepted belief that people who talk to themselves are strange or have some form of mental illness. This "condition" is something I would surely say many of us would try to avoid. The other thought might be, why bother if I don't believe what I am affirming? Like any exercise, the benefits will only come with repetition. We all know we will never have abs from doing sit ups for a day. Anyway, the take-home message: Affirmations work — and the most successful people use them. If I threw you a life jacket, would you grab it? *I just threw you one*.

In the next chapter, I give instructions on how to build your blueprint and how to use it. I will explain to you how to construct affirmations, where you can find them, and how to use them. I even have more good news: The blueprint for your perfect life includes food (keep reading).

Nutrition

I want to point out something to you right away: It does not say *diet*. We will change how you see this area of your life right now. Diet makes you think of restricting yourself and has a very bad word in it, *die*, which is something most people try to avoid. We want to change how you think of eating. From this point on, you fuel your body and add nutrients.

The definition of nutrition is: The sum of the process by which an animal or plant takes in and utilizes food substances. The great Jack Lalane once said, "If you got up every morning and gave your dog a doughnut, cigarette and cup of coffee, what would he look like?" It is funny that when analogies explain nutrition — people always nod their heads "yes." Like the one where you ask people if they had a Ferrari, would they put only the best oil, gas and fluids into it? Of course everyone says "yes." We use a car for 10 or maybe 20 years. Then why do we neglect to fuel our bodies, which now may last 100 years? People living to

100 are one of the largest growing populations in the United States and in many other countries.

What problem do we now have in fueling our bodies? We no longer eat food. In Michael Pollan's book, *In Defense of Food*, he explains that the food we put into our bodies give our bodies little or nothing of what we need to provide our bodies with nutrients. Don't believe me? Why as a society are we getting sicker and sicker — even with all the so-called medical advances? It's what we nutritionally do and do not put into our system.

How does this relate to our blueprint and constructing the framework for the life we hope to build for ourselves? Nutrition can be analogous to the material used to build a house. If we put inside the home's structure the best plumbing, electrical or lumber, the house will provide us with years of usefulness with little defect or need of repair. In fact, when you feed your body good nutrition to make a strong structure for your life, it becomes an area that begins to run on automatic pilot. When we have our ducks in a row in the area of nutrition, it improves our ability to work on other parts of our lives. On the flip side, poor Nutrition drags us down to a point where Exercise suffers, Self becomes more difficult, and Affirmations become less believable (SANE).

When we think of what we eat as fuel, exercise becomes easier and desirable. We're more motivated to work on the area of self and amplify our affirmation, because we like what we see in our mirrors. A great book written by a fellow colleague Dr. Eric Plasker titled *The 100 Year Lifestyle* begs the question, what would you do differently if you knew you were going to live a 100 years? I highly suggest you purchase his book and start asking yourself what you would change if you lived to a 100, because the chances of this happening are greater every day. We will cover some ideas of how to harmonize this part of the SANE structure of the blueprint with the other parts in the next chapter.

So remember the 21 days? This is super important when it comes to fueling our bodies. The changes you make in your nutritional intake over the first three weeks will spark you to charge into the next section, which is Exercise. The "E" word is scary for many of us until we learn the tricks to remove its teeth.

Exercise

Ah the best for last: Exercise. There is no need to go into the reasons why we need exercise. If you don't understand the importance of exercise, then "welcome" out of the cave in which you have been hiding. People use many excuses to avoid exercise. The two I commonly hear: It's hard and there's not enough time. First, everyone has enough time (there's always enough time if you make it a priority). The real problem people lack energy. The good news: We've already identified the area of nutrition as a way to improve our energy levels. Also, there is a secret to exercise, that only the super successful exercisers know. That's right, ladies and gentlemen, it's the morning. The morning is not only the key to getting your exercise in, but it's the key to starting the day off right. The first great thing about morning workouts — everyone else is asleep. What? Let me try and illustrate exactly what I mean.

The workouts that I find most often fail are the ones done after work or at night for many reasons. "The gym is too crowded." "I have to get home to my family." "That is the only time of the day I have to get things done." The excuses go on and on. To be quite honest, I had a lot of those issues, too, and agree with the pitfalls they create.

Now let's go back to the morning workout. The nice part is that we are only talking about getting up an hour early or maybe two. "But how will I get enough sleep?" The truth is we oversleep — and that often causes fatigue during the day. Gandhi only slept five hours a night. When we have things to do and we're inspired to do them, we get up. For example, people who like to go fishing or shop on the day after Thanksgiving find a way to get up.

Another nice aspect, especially if you have a family, is that while they're all sleeping, you get your workout in without neglecting anyone. The feeling you have of getting something done before most have woken up is empowering. All this information comes from someone who NEVER got up early and chanted the mantra that I needed eight hours of sleep a day. By saying this over and over to myself, my body started to believe it. Remember the power of self-talk? A study by Daniel Kripke, co director of research at the Scripps Clinic Sleep

Center in La Jolla, Calif., showed that people who sleep between 6.5 hr. and 7.5 hr. a night, as they report, live longest.[2] The study's results suggest you need around six hours and you'll be fine. And it will take about 21 days to get your body used to this.

Aha, but there is more. There is a metabolic advantage to working out in the morning. When you do your cardiovascular activity in the morning, that workout continues to work for you the rest of the day, turning up your metabolism. When we work out at night, as soon as we hit the pillow we lose that burst of metabolic advantage. Want to supercharge your morning routine? After your workout eat a real breakfast. When you do this, your body starts to burn energy and adds more to your metabolic advantage. So you actually begin to lose weight because you started eating earlier. Even better, when you eat a good breakfast in the morning you will consume fewer calories the rest of the day. People who eat a good, full breakfast in the morning eat fewer calories during the day and snack less. I hope this sheds some light on the fact that we have been doing everything backwards. I'm not saying all of you do this but my guess would be the majority are guilty. It's nice to know when to exercise — and we all know why we should be doing it, but how? You're asking the wrong question — the question is not "how" but "what."

What do I mean by "what?" When I say what, most people think I mean the activity. Should you do cardio or resistance training or stretching or Pilates? The truth is when it comes to exercise, at least for starters, do ANYTHING that you will at least do! The *act* of becoming *active* will lead to other *activities*. The road to success in any exercise program is what are you training for? When I say this, most people think about getting in shape, losing weight, yada, yada, yada. These are all results of working out and important reasons to do so.

Remember, goals are best achieved when they have meaning and a target date. Most workout programs fail because while workouts have the overall goal of health, they rarely have completion dates or benchmarks, which give you the answer to *what*. You need to have something to train for. Professional athletes

---

[2] "How Much Sleep Do You Really Need?", Laura Blue, Time in Partnership with CNN, www.time.com.

make incredible sacrifices and train at incredible levels in an effort to reach their ultimate goal with a target date.

The Olympics, the Super Bowl, the World Series — you will drastically increase your workout program's success when you attach it to some future event. Now I doubt many of you reading this will go for the Olympics. OK, so how about a vacation, a wedding or a family picture? If you went on two vacations a year, half a dozen weddings, and a party or two, that gives you almost a dozen reasons for training. So you conquer two areas: health and looks. You are becoming healthier by exercising and are looking better for future events. That's a win-win if I ever heard one.

In addition, you are positively affirming yourself by making a positive connection between exercises and how you look and feel. Also, think of all the positive affirmations others will give you at the party, wedding, or when they see the photos from your trip. Let me share with you the three steps on how to get up-to-speed with your exercise program.

"Nothing happens until something moves." — Albert Einstein

The first step is simple, get off your butt. Until this first step is achieved, there is no exercise that can be done. The second step is to do the one exercise you will do. Not the one everyone is doing, not the one you think is the one you *should* be doing, but the one you can tolerate doing on a consistent basis (21 days). Third, now that you are exercising, expand the boundaries of your exercise and find your first *what* to train for. There is nothing like a well-maintained house — a nice lawn, healthy garden and the message that a well-kept home conveys to visitors. Structure is not only what's on the inside but what's on the outside, too.

These are the parts of the SANE system within the blueprint. The SELF and AFFIRMATION sections are the fuel and workout for your brain. The NUTRITION and EXERCISE parts are the fuel and workout for your body. The brain and body must work together. When they are congruent, we are in a good place to achieve success. When they are on different pages, it can really hold us back. Now that you have the pieces of the blueprint for what you are trying to build, I can finally give you those *Tools* I have been talking about ... almost.

The Right *Tools* Tie it All Together

You are now beginning to realize how the blueprint attempts to incorporate many accepted areas of goal-setting and self-improvement. These time-tested strategies play a crucial role in building the life that you demand for yourself. In the process of using these methods myself I couldn't help but notice that for some people they didn't work. Many struggled with all the elements we have discussed, and I believed it was because they weren't all tied together. What if there was one page where someone could say, "Boom, here is a simple handy worksheet that encompasses what I want and who I am?" This is when I realized that you can have all the pieces to any project — a model plane, car engine or blueprint to a house — but these pieces mean nothing if you don't have the *Tools* to build them.

These *Tools* are the cornerstone of this book. I believe the *Tools* add the final element and tie it all together. These *Tools* are nothing new and have been around and used quite frequently. What makes them unique with regard to this book is how they incorporate into the blueprint and drastically increase your probability of success.

A major reason why I believe people fail even with proven methods — they don't have the necessary *Tools* to complete the job. It is almost impossible to change your life if you don't have your goals written out, and we now know from the vital areas in SANE that we need to cover all the bases. Goals are not enough; you need the proper *Tools* to help construct the plans called for on the blueprint and make them a reality. I have compiled a list of 110 *Tools* for you to choose from. They say give 110 percent of the vital information you need, so I thought it appropriate to give you 110 *Tools* — a virtual toolbox if you will.

Some you will use and some you won't. Some you will always use and some you never will. As I have strived to improve myself, I have compiled these from books, CDs, talks and even just life's experiences. I have done my best to give credit to those who deserve it. For many of them listed I believe it to be impossible to give any one person credit. Quite honestly, if you have done any work in this area, you know that common messages and themes are repeated over and over. What seems to differ from author to author is how to convey and implement these proven life lessons. This book takes the best of all worlds and puts it all together in a simple one-page sheet — a simple, easy-to-use blueprint.

In Chapter 4 you will be introduced to these *Tools*, which will tie the whole system together. They can almost be thought of as little words of advice to keep you on track for the rest of the blueprint. Every building or house has little accents and decor that make them unique. These details are similar to what these *Tools* offer. I've set up the blueprint to allow you to select six *Tools* that you believe enhance your probability in reaching your goals over the next 21 days. These *Tools* also cover a myriad of different realms. One *Tool* in particular allows inventing a *Tool* of your own. You may naturally want to take a peek at what some of them are; please go ahead. You've perhaps already glanced over them. To be quite honest, reading these *Tools* alone will give you a leg up on having a happier and successful life.

When you look at the *Tools,* they fall into many categories from headspace to health. There will be a few that have been around for years but are still great ones, just like a classic song or car that never goes out of style. We call those oldies but goodies (OBG) and when it comes to the *Tools* in this book, I put a little OBG by them.

Just like the real world, some tools can perform more than one job. This situation is no different than the *Tools* I am about to provide you to maximize success with your blueprint. Some of the 110 *Tools* can double up as affirmations. We call these kinds of *Tools* "Power Tools" because they pack a bigger punch. They can be used in the *Tool* section or as an affirmation in the SANE section. For example, you may use *Tool 19, Positive thinking always works better than negative thinking*. This is a great *Tool* to help us work toward all the aspects of SANE on our blueprint. It can also be used in the affirmation section of SANE to be repeated and retrain our way of thinking.

Sometimes you need a specialized *Tool*. I call these "Specialty Tools," and the 110 also contain some of those insights. Since Specialty Tools can also be used as goals, they can also be used in the SANE's goal sections, too. For example, you may use *Tool 10, Get up earlier*. This can be used in the *Tool* section as a strategy to reach your goals in the SANE section. On the other hand, you may enter it in the Self section as one of your goals to achieve over the next 21 days. Remember,

Mission Statement

_____

_____

_____

_____

_____

1 2 3 4 5 6 7 8 9 10 11 12 13 14 15 16 17 18 19 20 21

I.   II.   III.

IV.   V.   VI.

Self:

Affirmation:

"

"

Nutrition:

Exercise:

Tools:

1.

2.

3.

4.

5.

6.

X _____

there are no wrong answers to working on your life except for doing no work at all. If you want to know what your life will look like five years from now, continue doing nothing and leave your blueprint blank.

X Marks the Spot

You'll notice in the last diagram, which illustrates the entire blueprint template, there is a section with an X at the bottom right which requires your signature. I've provided this for a simple reason — it symbolizes your commitment to what you have written down. All your life you have been asked to sign things to acknowledge whatever is being asked of you. I find this symbolic gesture to be important, because it has been wired into your subconscious. Many people sign things without reading the contract. What differs here is that you wrote the contract.

Well, I've just explained the blueprint. You've just read all of my beliefs wrapped up in a system on how you can give your life the guidance it needs to reach the levels of success you hope to achieve. There is one catch to the whole system that is under your complete control: DOING IT. *Tool 44 states, The definition of insanity is doing the same thing over and over and expecting a different outcome.* If what you are doing is not working, then try the blueprint and let's get going. If what you are trying is nothing, then we already know why it's not working. *Tool 21 reads, Life is a game, there are many ways to play but you play to win.* You are playing the game right now whether you like it or not. I just handed you a playbook on how to increase the level of wins and the strategies to avoid losses. It is all up to you, as *Tool 36* says, *No decision is a decision.*

Chapter 3:
The Instructions

"Do not go where the path may lead. Go instead where there is no path and leave a trail."

— Author Unknown

So let's say you buy a brand new barbeque, you get the thing home and pour all the pieces onto the floor. A good chance exists that you might be able to put it together. Most likely, when you try doing this (without reading the instructions) you have a few extra pieces still lying around. Not a great idea when you are about to mix propane and fire in a confined space. This situation is no different when it comes to putting together your life. There is a problem though. When it comes to having a happy, successful life, you're never given a set of plans, instructions or *Tools*. You have now been given all the components of that blueprint, the problem is the pieces are scattered around the living-room floor. On top of which, your head may feel a little scrambled. Never fear, because I am about to give you the instructions on how to put your first blueprint for life together.

First things first, you need a blank blueprint to start working on. There are two ways to accomplish this: First, copy the one located on page 35 of this book. I suggest you enlarge it to fit an 8 ½ by 11 page. If you are Internet-savvy that's even better. Go to www.BeTheHammerNotTheNail.com and print one right from the site in its originally intended size and form. It's best to make multiple copies since this will be your first blueprint and you also will rewrite your sheet in the coming weeks. Next grab your pen, any color will do. If you're anything like me, I like to use a four-color pen to make the four different sections you will complete stand out. For now, just grab your favorite writing utensil to make composing your plan feel most comfortable. Then proceed with Step 1 and get started!

Hold on one second, though, some words of advice. This process may be the first time you've created a blueprint or a life plan or it might be your 10th; but anyone new to my process will experience this system for the first time. New things often feel weird, different or uncomfortable and we often try to avoid these feelings. Just give it a test drive. If you have previously worked on goals and affirmations, think of this as a new technique to add to your repertoire. If this is your first experience with a "self-help book," then congrats you have come this far. Since you bought a book on the subject and made it to the third chapter, I will assume you've already experienced personal growth and come one step closer to your life goals. Lastly, allow me to emphasize the need to be honest with yourself. If an architect does not put full thought into his or her blueprint, the house has the potential to be flawed or fall apart. If you are not focused and truthful about what you want, then your blueprint may not produce the desired result.

Step 1: Laying the Foundation

OK, first things first … *you*. You must build your foundation to set the theme for the whole blueprint, which is the first part of the *Be the Hammer Not the Nail* system and the first thing that you will be reading when you go over your blueprint each day. Remember, we discussed earlier that companies use a mission statement to define who they are, who they want to be, and how they go about achieving these beliefs. Holding yourself accountable to your mission statement helps all the other parts of your blueprint fall into place. Also, by having your blueprint posted in three to four areas that you visit daily, others are bound to see it. Putting your blueprint in full view for others to see helps make you accountable and further your resolve to be rooted in what your mission statement set forth.

I have put together three simple exercises that you can perform to help create your mission statement. Over time, as things change and develop, your mission statement will change. When you get a good one that really works, it can stay the same for some time. When this occurs, this is good — it means you poured a sturdy, solid foundation that needs little if any repairs. So let's back up the cement truck and let's get to work.

The Power of Your Words

"Sticks and stones might break my bones but words will never hurt me." You've all heard that phrase since childhood. The truth is that words are very powerful, and you should carefully choose the ones you select to describe yourself. That is the first assignment to complete in writing your first mission statement — to compile a list of words that you think best describes you. Make your list also describe who you want to be. Sample words I am talking about include integrity, pride, respect, love, drive, personality, dreams, focus and so on. Do the words that people use to describe you match the words you choose for yourself? The obvious goal is to get the two in sync. I recommend you put the book down and start with 10 words that you would like to represent you.

Now that you have compiled a list of words that you want to represent you, you come up with a way to make those words work in your favor. In this next section, I would like you to come up with some phrases that will help give these words power and strength. Following are some examples of what I am talking about: "I will give my best ..." "I will strive to be ..." "I will ..." "By doing this I can..." "I know by doing ... I can achieve ..." "I am about ..." Remember, there are no right or wrong answers.

You try to take the words you have chosen to mold, form and construct them into phrases and sentences to develop a mission statement that supports any house, building or life. For a simple start, just use "I will ..." Looking back at mine in the second chapter, you can see that this is how I started my first mission statement. Now stop reading and start writing some "I will ..." You will discover a few more possible directions that you didn't think about when picking some of your words.

A mission statement should be comprised of all the things that are most important to you. When all the important areas of your life are identified and congruent, then achievement of your goals and ability to reach new levels of success become easier. I want you to think of all the things most important to you in your life. For example, to serve others, be the best parent, God, charity, growth, wealth, spirituality, etc. What is most important to you? Remember, you will read this mission statement many times so it will remind you of where to focus. Areas that you feel you have neglected in the past will be more in the forefront of your mind. By taking this action daily, pitfalls and distractions to success become more bridled and offer less of a chance of sidetracking you from your goals and ultimate success. Take a minute to write down the things that are most important to you and then let's put it all together.

You now have, in my opinion all the parts to write a first (or maybe not) working mission statement. I have limited the space on your blueprint for a reason. Make it to the point and simple enough that you will read it every morning and every night. If you write too many pages, it will never get read and hence serve no purpose. Going back to my first mission statement, it would have never fit in our blueprint system and to be honest, it was too long to be useful on a daily basis. Here is my present mission statement.

My mission is to make the absolute most that I can of my life. I can do this best by serving others. I will take care of my body. I will do my best to incorporate God into my life. I will give 100%. When I live each day with integrity, pride, respect and love, there is nothing I can't achieve.

Now take all three areas that you just worked on and write a paragraph that will serve as the foundation for your life. Write something that as you read it, you say to yourself, "If I become this person and lead my life this way, there is no level of happiness that I cannot achieve." That's basically the bottom line for the whole system. Building a blueprint for your life to reach your goals, hitting the levels of success you desire, and ultimately having all the happiness you could hope for out of life. Now go mix that cement and start to pour your foundation so you can get on with the rest of the plans/blueprint.

Step 2: Target Dates and Inspections

Now that you have written your mission statement, you have a solid foundation for your structure. You have the ability to start building — and building a house is a process similar to building your life. You must build some parts first before going on to construct other areas. If you came to a worksite every day, you would want to know what was being built. Plans would be posted all around the worksite to inform you exactly how to construct something. These plans would have deadlines that particular areas needed to be finished by so other areas could be started. The final phase would require an inspection of the areas to ensure they properly work. If they are, the building process can continue as planned. If they are not, new plans must be written to fix the problem and get the house back on track. Without these critical inspections, the building process becomes stalled, or even worse the house becomes flawed or defective — and that can lead to more difficult problems to fix down the road.

Let's start looking at how you will use the 21 days provided by the blueprint. You first need to decide what day to begin construction, meaning what day will be the first day you use your blueprint. My best suggestion: Make day one a Monday, and then at the end of the 21-day period you will finish your sheet on a Sunday. This approach allows you to start on a Monday, which kicks off most work weeks, thus allowing you from day one of a new week to incorporate new goals that you may have added and possibly test a new affirmation and freshly selected *Tools*. I also recommend this Sunday end date for your 21-day cycle, which will give you time to review everything. If your work week is different or if it changes now and then, start on your preferred day. I honestly don't believe it makes much difference what day you select. You want to maximize the first day and save time to inspect your plan on the last day.

On the worksite of our life, you work every day. No day off exists from life — and you have to work daily if you want to achieve success. First copy the blueprint and put it in multiple areas of the worksite. I recommend areas such as the fridge, bathroom, your shirt or back pocket, office, car, locker and so on. Three or four spots around the house work well and then you have what the plan calls for located in multiple areas for ongoing reference.

Every morning start by reading the entire sheet and do so once again right before bedtime. This reminds you about what you are building each day. Each new day you become consciously aware of what you need to do — and you remind yourself before sleep and put your subconscious mind to work. How nice, you can build on your plan while you sleep!

I also encourage you to read your affirmation at least 10 times per day. You want to try to install this mantra in the worksite. Use it as the motto for the work you do on your "life site." Finally, I suggest that whenever you pass your blueprint, give it the onceover.

If you get something from the fridge, give it a glance. If you brush your teeth, give it the onceover. By using your sheet as a target and a reminder, you are less likely to stray off course. You are more likely to build the "life house" that the plans call for.

Before you can start working on new areas, you need to do inspections and find what areas are working and what areas need a little repair. At the end of the 21 days you will be writing a new blueprint, but you need the old one to help assist in constructing one that will get the next phase of the "life house" focused and working properly. First, you will start by checking the foundation (your mission statement) to see if there are any cracks or sagging parts. Then you will rewrite your mission statement to shore up problem areas. If the foundation is solid and holds up, then leave it alone.

You will next analyze your short- and long-term goals. See what works, what doesn't, and adjust accordingly. Check your affirmation to make sure that it is the best mantra or motto for your building's current phase. Finally, make sure you select the appropriate *Tools* to help you build what the new blueprint calls for. During different phases in your building process, the *Tools* you need change. When you do the things listed here, you constantly re-aim your scope at the target — and when you do this, you can celebrate many more wins. To be a good foreman of your life, you must know what works and what doesn't. You must keep the work focused on what is the goal and ensure that the plan can be built by having the best *Tools* for the job. As the "boss" of your life, you have to be present, stay on top of the details, and build your "structure" the best you can. Now let's take a moment and dream about all the things you want to do to the house in the future.

Step 3: Long-Term Projects

In all my time of seeing new home construction, I have never seen the pool and garden put in before the walls, plumbing and electrical work; however, you should know what you want in the yard and where the "pool" and "garden" should eventually go, but first things first. The two work hand-in-hand, working on the immediate needs of the house while always remembering where to add the extraneous things you'd like to do later.

So the long-term projects actually fit into two categories: the long-term goals that you would like to achieve this year; and future dreams you have for your life that, when appropriate, you hope to go for and achieve.

Six Roman numerals are blank on your blueprint. These do not all have to be filled out and conversely this number doesn't limit you. I think it works since it allows a nice balance between long-term goals you work toward for the year and future aspirations that you want to keep on the horizon. So to make things simple, let's use three for long-term goals you hope to achieve before the end of the year and three ambitions you want to keep fresh in your mind.

The long-term goals may be things like a target weight, the number of sales you hope to reach, or grades that you hope to achieve. When you identify ones that you would like to reach this year, you simply enter them in the Roman numeral spots. Then, when you work on the SANE part of the system later in the chapter, you target necessary areas that you need to make these long-term goals become reality.

I love that this area allows you to get a little bit adventurous. You can write down things that may be a real reach for you or something that is way out of your comfort zone. For me, I put that I would like to do some acting one day. This is a crazy dream of mine that if it happens, great, but if it doesn't, no big deal; but by writing it down I never let myself forget, and if the opportunity arises, I am much more likely to see it. For you it may be an exotic dream vacation — one that you don't need this year but maybe you will take in five years. I guarantee that placing your long-term goal in this area drastically increases its likelihood of coming to fruition.

You shouldn't be afraid to let this area be fluid. Sometimes you may have a lot to work on and all the spots will be for things you are trying to reach in the coming year. It is also possible that you are in a good place that allows you to fantasize a little more freely. If this is the case, go wild with four or five spots in the Roman numeral section. There should always be at least one or two that your SANE section is striving to reach. Keep in mind, people may look at these and that's great; the more people that know, the more likelihood that they can become reality. Remember, we never arrive; we always have work and repair to do. With that said, keep this section in check accordingly.

Step 4: Structure and Framework

A house has thousands of things that make it become a home and for the most part, no two houses are really alike. A life has thousands of things that comprise it and it is these differences that make us individuals. When you step back from a home and look at it, there are some basic things that make it a house, which means you can take a house to its simplest form to describe what makes it so. It has walls and a roof, windows and doors, electrical and plumbing. You can all agree these are the things you have come to expect when you consider what makes up a house. To make a system useable when working on our own life, you must have one that is simple without sacrificing the basics needed to reach the success you expect. I have made this as straightforward as possible to get you in SANE.

I already introduced all the players in the SANE system. Once again, they are Self, Affirmation, Nutrition and Exercise. These areas, when focused and congruent, can take you wherever you want to go. All you are is mind and body. The Self and Affirmation work mainly with the mind while the Nutrition and Exercise work mainly on your body. When this structure and framework for your life is peaked and at an optimal level and focused on short- and long-term goals, everything points in one direction. So what you enter in these sections are short-term goals that you wish to accomplish within the next 21 days or established goals you hope to continue. By doing so, you will reach your long-term goals, short-term goals, and you will keep on a path of established goals you wish to affirm. The goals listed in this section not only serve to help you reach your destination, but they also help you avoid pitfalls along your journey.

"If you aim at nothing, you hit it every time."

SELF. I describe self as all the things that make you you. It acts as a personal compass to point in the right direction — where you want to go. When not focused or written down, things that comprise you and your life go in 8,000 directions. You will give this chaos direction in this section, and it will address all areas — family, career, health, finances, education, recreation, charity, adventure, travel, romance, relationships, spiritual. You have the opportunity to pick from these areas and write down the direction of where you want it all to go.

The experts say with goal setting you need to be specific, write it down, and apply a deadline. Don't worry our program has the deadline set, which is every 21 days. You write everything down on your blueprint. The specificity depends on you. If this is new to you, I suggest you keep it simple to make some wins and get success under your belt; however, the feeling of winning may be new to you. The great news though: winning begets winning. So develop a taste for it because it tastes good. If you need a kick start in this area, just list four to five things you have been procrastinating on. Also, keep around that number, give or take a few. After you feel like you have your SELF goals written down, let's move to the next section.

AFFIRMATION. You now know the importance of affirmations from Chapter 2. You might not realize there are common everyday affirmations all around us. At most sites where home construction occurs, it becomes common to see signs that say "Safety First" or "Think Safety." Such affirmation offer mantras for that site. The foreman tries to set an attitude and a mindset for the work being performed there. With regard to the blueprint you are constructing for your life, you will use the same thought process. You want to choose an affirmation that will set the tone for what you build. If you're a company, it would be your motto. There are a ton of books out there for finding or developing affirmations. One that I like is *The Winners Journal* by John and Pam Carls. The authors provide daily affirmations, and it also has many other *Tools* for you to read and work on.

This helpful publication also provides another secret — a section with exercises to assist with your mission statement. When you get to *Tool 76* in Chapter 4, I give you all the information you need on where to find this gem (which I also have used for years now).

Here is a list to get you started:

I set goals and make plans to reach them.

Goals give me direction.

I do my best all the time.

I will improve myself in all areas of my life.

I ask and I shall receive.

I consult winners for winning ideas.

I increase the quality and quantity of my services.

I reach my goals because I stay on track.

I win because I am persistent.

I will grow and move beyond my present circumstances.

I will learn from every situation, good or bad.

I avoid negative people and negative events.

I welcome opportunities to serve others.

I meet all challenges with determination.

I refuse to accept defeat.

I learn something good from every person with whom I come in contact.

My enthusiasm adds zest and pleasure to my life.

If I act enthusiastic then I'll be enthusiastic.

How I think determines how I act.

I judge each day not by the harvest, but by the seeds I plant.

I give to life what I want life to give to me.

I translate my visions into realities.

I realize the value of sincere appreciation.

My affirmations help me reach my goals.

I win because I believe I can.

I inspire others into action by communicating from the heart.

I bring out the best in others.

I dream of things that never were and ask why not.

I let go of old ideas so new ones can enter.

I learn something from everyone.

I thank everyone who makes my day go better.

The road to success is always under construction (my favorite).

Tomorrow's results start today (what I am using right now).

I was inspired just writing these down. I hope you have been inspired by reading them. I took these from the journal mentioned above, but there are myriad of resources to find affirmations. An affirmation is a thought you try to implant deep into your conscious and subconscious mind. The majority of successful people use them. Those successful people who don't are in the minority. I would say it is much more likely they don't realize they are doing it or might even be a tad embarrassed to say that they do. Many with oversized egos would like you to believe it just "comes natural" to them. At any rate, start working on what will be the first affirmation for your first blueprint.

NUTRITION. To get the most out of a home, you obviously want to fortify it with the best materials possible. To get the most out of it, you need to build smart. If you do so, it will respond by being the home of your dreams and lasting a lifetime. When you cut corners and neglect this important step, you will encounter problems along the way. In turn, you won't be able to build an optimal home that can weather storms and challenges. No matter how much work you put into other areas of the building process, using inferior materials will always hold you back. In addition, if you don't pay attention to this crucial step in building, you will constantly be spending time to repair these areas. When the house constantly looks tired and falling apart, how can you spend time reaching goals you have for other areas of the home? What you feed your home ultimately affects in large part what the house can become and ultimately affects the success of the other crucial areas of the building project.

I think you all understand what I'm talking about. How you feel physically when you properly fill your body with the best nutrients possible will increase the probability of success. It will increase the probability of reaching our goals. Now there are certain things that will be constant for most of us, vitamins, fruits and vegetables, etc. Then there are things that will differ from person to person depending upon what our ultimate plan calls for; but the bottom line is that you need to write down what your goals are for nutrition and what you want to put into your body.

Once again, I'm not coming up with some new secret. You all know you feel better when you are healthy. You're more likely to do things when you're not tired, sluggish or just feeling rundown. You accomplish the most when you are feeling your best, and to feel your best you need to put the best into your body. This doesn't mean going crazy. I think most would agree if 90 percent of a home was built with great materials, you could have a few spots that didn't have the BEST. A doorknob in the garage does not have to be the best or most expensive available. What I'm trying to say is, you can have a treat now and then as long as you keep it in the boundaries of your goals. Some examples to help you get started:

No Candy

More Vegetables

No late night eating

No snacking

Eat breakfast

No caffeine

Drink more water

Only 2,000 calories a day

Eat dinner with the family every night

No fast food

Pack my lunch for work/school

I'm not saying any of these are RIGHT or the ones that you should choose. I am trying to show you what they should look like in this section. If you are like many, you may be totally lost in what is right for you in this section. If I was building a house, I wouldn't know what the BEST materials are. So if you feel this way, do some homework or get with a professional who can help get you started in this section. If you have difficulty reaching the level of success you are hoping to attain, it might simply be because you are not fueling your success properly.

EXERCISE. A great home needs three things: strength, endurance and flexibility. You want a home that is strong and that can support all the things that you have planned for it (muscle). You want it to have a good endurance system that will be able to last over the long haul (cardio). You want it to be able to bend and twist but not break (stretching). When you have a nice combination of all these things, the house will take you where you want to go and will be able to endure all the things that are thrown its way. These things, once again, will vary from home to home. A combination of these things will be quite different in a beach house versus a cabin located in the snow and mountains. An office building will be built very differently from an apartment, condo or home. One thing is for sure, the characteristics mentioned above determine the ultimate success of any of these structures.

Many years ago, you didn't have to put a lot of thought into these things. You gained them all naturally from daily activities that you performed for day-to-day life. You ran after food and ran away from predators (cardio). You carried water, game and produce to be prepared and consumed (muscle). To be honest, with regard to flexibility, I'm not sure mankind lived long enough for that to really matter in the past, but since you live three times as long, I know it matters now. Fast forward to modern day, it would be obvious to say that for the most part you don't naturally get these things. People these days need to become "urban athletes." What I mean by this is that you need to do your day-to-day jobs and activities AND THEN find a way to incorporate the things that your body needs to be successful. In this section I define success as longevity and to do so in a way that is graceful and allows the greatest probability of achievement. I mentioned this differs for all of us, but the equation is the same. To clarify, you need a form of all three but how you fill in those blanks will differ. All the research continues to illustrate the same three things:

1. You need to build muscle mass - Resistance Training
2. You need to build endurance - Cardiovascular Training
3. You need to keep a flexible frame - Joint Flexibility/Muscular Compliance

There are many opinions on importance and how to get there, but I would challenge anyone who says these three areas don't play an important role in overall health and the ability to thrive and achieve success. If you're like most, you need a little proof. With regard to muscle mass, it plays a large role in mobility and performance in our later years. You need to build muscle to deal with problems and challenges that may arise down the road.

A modern day example is those that have heart surgery. In the old days, patients would rest in bed for days, losing muscle drastically in something called "bed rest de-conditioning." Fast forward to today and they will have a patient out of bed and at least standing after a bypass surgery, thus causing leg muscles to fire and save them from wasting away. Cardiovascular conditioning (i.e., raising your heart rate) has been proven to be crucial for many areas, including weight management, lower risk of cancer and a decreased probability of countless pathologies. Lastly, joint mobility and flexibility illustrate a decrease in morbidity. One specific study suggests that greater "hunching over" with increased age correlates to higher levels of heart and lung pathologies. Even with all of these examples, does anyone question the quality of life when all these areas are met? Let's look at some possibilities for this section:

Brisk Walking

Running

Aerobics

Bike Riding

Rowing

Weight Training

Pilates

Circuit Training

Massage

Yoga

Chiropractic

Rock Climbing

Any sport you can imagine

Let's be very clear in this section. None of these activities alone make you successful or give you the life of your dreams — they are simply a part of the plan to ensure success. Is it such a stretch to believe that if you improve in these areas, it will help you achieve what you hope to accomplish? Not to mention what healthy habits and attitudes will open for you. Having goals to reach in this area of your life will make the other areas of the SANE system congruent, thus enhancing the probability of achieving what your plan calls to build. By this point you have established the importance of building what you want. This is best accomplished when all the areas of the plan are on the same page and headed in the same direction. These areas of goal setting, in my opinion, help you get where you want to go. Experts have identified and amplified all these areas in some variation. The importance of these areas of SANE is well-established. If you accept this, then why aren't people doing them? I believe these areas need to be built and building requires *Tools*.

Step 5: Picking the Right *Tools* for the Job

If you have followed the instructions up to this point, your blueprint should almost be complete. You have laid the foundation for yourself. You have established the mission statement of who you want to be and how you want to be. You have laid out a timeframe to accomplish your goals and then an end date to review and refine your goals. You have future paced yourself, identifying long-term goals for yourself with some crazy dreams sprinkled in the mix. You have written down Short-term goals and a mantra to parallel these goals, knowing that having all the parts of the SANE section complete will give you direction and focus. These time-tested and established techniques successful people implement and used by professionals who teach these skills and demand their students use. With that said, I pose the question again that I did earlier, why doesn't doing these time-tested truths translate into success for all of us? Because you can only build what the plan calls for if you have *Tools* to build.

Herein lies one of the major components of this book and how the system was born. Having targets to shoot for is crucial, but you can only shoot at these targets if you have the *Tools* to assist you in that effort. A target is only a target without a bow and arrow. I found that you all know that you need to shoot at goals to reach, but I, like most of you, fell short. I needed something to help me hit my target.

In the following chapter, I listed 110 *Tools* that you will choose from to make your goals become reality. They are there to help you build what your plan requires you to do. Some of them are obvious and ones you know and have heard a million times before. Many will be new to you. There will also be some that you will never use. Over time you will even develop some *Tools* of your own.

At this point, I want you to put your sheet aside and read through Chapter 4. After you have done so, you will choose six *Tools* that you believe will solidify your ability to build your blueprint. After reading these I truly believe you will transform what you know you should be doing to actually doing it. Upon reading Chapter 4 and completing your blueprint, you will sign your sheet on the bottom line and then continue to work your plan and continue to build. The road to success is always under construction, but NOTHING has ever been built without a plan and without the proper *Tools* to build what that plan calls for. Now go find YOUR *Tools* and build YOUR plan for a successful life.

Chapter 4:
The *Tools*

1.   *Don't major in minor things.*

2.   *Take time to think. Take time for yourself.*

3.   *Accept change as part of life; don't fight it.*

4.   *We are products of our past, we don't have to be prisoners of it.*

5.   *Be grateful for the things you have and give thanks.*

6.   *The five-minute rule.*

7.   *Stop and smell the roses. OBG*

8.   *Make a board of directors.*

9.   *What would a Hall of Famer do?*

10.   *Get up earlier.*

11.   *Smile first and see the reaction you get from others.*

12.   *You never get a second chance at a first impression. OBG*

13.   *Readers are leaders, one book a week.*

14.   *Pray.*

15.   *Pick a charity.*

16.   *Make a dream board.*

17.   *Become a better listener.*

18.   *Turn off the TV.*

19.   *Positive thinking always works better than negative thinking.*

20. *Connect the rings.*

21. *Life is like a game, there are different ways to play but you play to win.*

22. *There is only one group of people who don't have problems, dead people.*

23. *If I talked to you the way you talked to yourself, you'd hate me.*

24. *Review the wins you have each week.*

25. *Don't let your music die inside of you. What music do you have to play?*

26. *Effective leaders lead by example.*

27. *Surround yourself with growth-oriented people.*

28. *Eat with your head days one through six, eat with your heart on day seven.*

29. *211 vs. 212*

30. *Turn your cell phone off for 24 hours.*

31. *Winners make commitments, losers make promises.*

32. *The hole you receive through is only as big as the hole you give through.*

33. *What you think most of is what you become.*

34. *Walk to conclusions.*

35. *The road of "someday" leads to the town of "nowhere."*

36. *No decision is a decision.*

37. *Get in the habit of sending thank you notes.*

38. *On the road of change there will be many tempting places to park;
    clearly define your enemy to growth.*

39. *Live each day as your last knowing you'll live to 100.*

40. *If your tool is a hammer, don't make everything a nail.*

41. *You have to be there mentally before you are there physically.*

42. *The four-minute mile.*

43. *The baby elephant at the circus.*

44. *The definition of "insanity" is doing the same thing over and over and ex-
    pecting a different outcome.*

45. *A short pencil is better than a long memory.*

46. *The best investment you will ever make is in your mind.*

47. *Garbage in, garbage out. Good stuff in, good stuff out.*

48. *Start each day with a GOOD breakfast.*

49. *Do I really need this?*

50. *Language is not only spoken; what are you saying?*

51. *Be on time, don't be late. OBG*

52. *The road to success is always under construction.*

53. *For those who believe, no proof is needed and for those who don't, no proof is enough.*

54. *Track your progress; update your resume or curriculum vitae regularly.*

55. *Stop comparing yourself to other people.*

56. *Ask yourself, what's the flipside?*

57. *When you're ready to quit, remember Yo Pal Hal.*

58. *Join the "Why Not Club."*

59. *Live your life like it was on TV.*

60. *"Don't think it only hurts the ballclub."*

61. *When the rope gets slippery, tie a knot and hang on.*

62. *Happy people work on solutions, unhappy people talk about problems.*

63. *The problem is not in making mistakes; it is in making the same mistake over and over and over.*

64. *Stop being realistic.*

65. *Rich people believe "I create my life." Poor people believe "Life happens to me."*

66. *Become more selfish.*

67. *Compile a team of experts.*

68. *Start remembering people's names.*

69. *Choose the latté or a million dollars.*

70. *Keep an open mind.*

71. *Sharpen your axe.*

72. *It takes an hour to burn 500 calories; it takes seconds to eat 500.*

73. *Five percent of the population will disagree with you no matter what.*

74. *Be a Johnny Today.*

75. *Blood is NOT thicker than water.*

76. *Keep a Journal.*

77. *Laughter is one of the keys to life.*

78. *Learn a new definition each day.*

79. *Be a student and a teacher.*

80. *An All-Star in baseball fails seven out of 10 times.*

81. *You don't want it bad enough!*

82. *"I worried about a lot of things, half of which never happened."*
    — Mark Twain

83. *Stop stomping on sandcastles.*

84. *Listen to motivational CDs.*

85. *Ultimately, you choose.*

86. *You can put some people up in a castle and they will complain the floors are made out of stone.*

87. *Stop acting your age.*

88. *Form a Master Mind Group.*

89. *Keep in touch.*

90. *Get a theme song.*

91. *I am not alone.*

92. *Dress for success. OBG*

93. *Make a superhero.*

94. *Find your alternative.*

95. *Stop reading the newspaper and tabloids.*

96. *Make gossip positive.*

97. *You will always remember what came hard and mostly forget what came easy.*

98. *Never settle for anything less than you are capable of achieving.*

99. *To eat an elephant, you cut it into little pieces.*

100. *Focus on yourself.*

101. *The will to win is nothing compared to the will to prepare to win.*

102. *The best cure for a sluggish mind is to disturb its routine.*

103. *Supplementation is a must.*

104. *Get a Coach.*

105. *Celebrate your flaws.*

106. *To get what you've never had, you must do what you've never done.*

107. *Get a lucky charm.*

108. *I want to be more like_____.*

109. *Insert your Tool here.*

110. *It's not what happens to you, it's what you do with what happens to you.*

1. Don't major in minor things.

How many people do you know who have a bachelor's degree in minor things? Do you see the connection in your life when you focus on minor versus major things? It's no wonder people claim they don't have enough time these days. What a waste to spend a large amount of time or energy on something that doesn't warrant it. Just think about how silly that even sounds. By spending an inordinate amount of time and energy on something that doesn't need it, you deprive time for the major things that actually require effort. In addition, by spending so much effort on minor things, it makes the major things just look that much *more* major. Practical use of this *Tool* comes easy and fast. Pretty soon you will take a quick pause before a problem occurs and figure out what category it belongs in, and thus, allow more time for bigger/major challenges, which in turn, don't seem as major. Minor things can be resolved quicker and free up time to tackle the big issues.

Don't sweat the small stuff and it's all small stuff is a great book by Richard Hyperion. OK, maybe it's not *all* small stuff, but consider all the small things we make such a big deal over. When I first heard this, I discovered that when you start making a big deal out of little things, you start making a big deal about *everything*. Another problem with making a big deal out of everything, others don't know what is a big deal or what isn't.

When I started using this *Tool*, a couple of interesting things happened. First, I was able to separate the important from the not so important. Second, when I did call my shot about something important, others knew it was something important, because I didn't make a big deal of *everything* and what I got in turn were people helping me respond to the things that were *important* and needed to be addressed.

2. Take time to think. Take time for yourself.

Think about it. Sorry, bad joke. When was the last time you really took some time and thought about things? I think most of us do not take time to go somewhere and just think. My suggestion would be to find a thinking place — a park, room, lake or even a curb will do; anywhere you feel comfortable to do some *thinking*. If you pick the same place, it will become a good routine. Make it uninterrupted time where you can be alone. This is time for you to reflect and evaluate. If you do this, you will find that the things that seem like big challenges won't be that bad. Also, you will have peace of mind knowing that when a problem does arise, you will have your daily "thinking" time to go over it. Instead of freaking out when something comes up, you can relax a bit knowing there is time to contemplate later.

When you start making this a routine, the next step is to take it to the next level, which uses meditation. Now when many hear the word "meditation," they get a little freaked out. Meditation is really just the opposite of taking time to think. *What?* What I mean is meditation is the practice of clearing your mind, which is hard to do. It takes practice and with practice, you will get better. As you start to clear your mind and think of nothing, it may be only for a few seconds in the beginning, but eventually that will turn to minutes. When you master the ability to clear your thoughts and mind, you will gain strength in letting go of things that clutter your brain. If you don't buy all that, simply accept the proven benefits of stress relief, lower blood pressure, and a longer healthier life.

3. Accept change as part of life; don't fight it.

This could be one of the most important *Tools* in the bag. I would compare it to a screwdriver or a hammer, something that you should be able to find in every house and toolbox. It surprises me how many people have difficulty with change, including myself at one time. It may be one of the biggest areas that hinder personal growth. One of the best examples of this aversion to change involves people who never get over an ex or a divorce. Years later it still consumes them.

Let's admit change feels uncomfortable, weird and unfamiliar — all feelings that most try to avoid. The funny thing is that change is a part of life; it's going to happen. You can either embrace it or wait for things to go back to the way they were. Waiting for things to go back to the way they used to be (which almost never happens) leaves you waiting, waiting and waiting — and what happens? *Nothing.* No personal growth or development; we just sit there and if we're not growing, we're dying. Want to know what your life will look like five years from now? Keep doing exactly what you are doing now.

Accept change as a part of life, a part of growing. If you find this area to be a major struggle in your life and would like to learn more, I highly suggest you read *Who Moved My Cheese* by Spencer Johnson. This book offers an almost perfect example of why I wrote *Be the Hammer Not the Nail.* Before I read Spencer's book I simply didn't have a *Tool* to deal with change. Now I do — and now so do you.

4. We are products of our past, we don't have to be prisoners of it.

I discovered this *Tool* in a book called *The Purpose Driven Life* by Rick Warren. We all have pasts; we all have a few bones in the closet. Those bones only become skeletons when we decide to put all the bones together and give them life. What I am trying to say is that our past does not have to dictate who we are or where we go. It can guide us where we want to go by knowing where we don't want to return to.

I hear the excuse that others won't let me forget my past. Well, I am here to tell you that that is kind of up to you. Responding or reacting to the acknowledgement of the past feeds it and allows those skeletons to dance. These aspects of our past are not always bad. Sometimes we had great pasts; we were at the top in the past. We may be having difficulty living up to what we were or what we used to be. Only one person holds the key to that closet and that is you.

The people and stories that I like to celebrate are the ones that have the past that most could not overcome but did. Those are the kind of stories that inspire and motivate. Those are the kind of stories that show how leaders are born. If you are going to use the problems in your closet as an excuse (that may actually be the size of a small bedroom), then it might be better to go lock yourself inside, because that is what you do when you let the past hinder growth, goals and love. When you reach your goals and new heights in spite of past problems, it feels good. When you rise above "bone and chain," you provide an inspirational example to give others the strength to do the same. Give yourself and others the gift of the ability to break the bear traps used to hold you down is one of the most powerful experiences I know.

5. Be grateful for the things you have and give thanks.

"You don't know what you've got till it's gone." I believe it was the glam rock hair band of the 1990s, Cinderella that made a hit song out of that quote. This *Tool* truly reminds us of the things we take for granted. Our health, shelter and food, these are things we expect to be automatic; therefore, we never take the time to be grateful for them. As we grow accustomed to all the luxuries around us, like clean running water, the ability to purchase food 24 hours a day, or the ability to watch 500 channels on TV, we forget about all the things we have. Instead we focus on all the things we don't have. Just by sheer mathematics there will always be more things you don't have than you do. The key point: Even if you have more things, they are still just things; you are not going to take a moving truck to your funeral.

When you start to use this *Tool*, be aware of all that you do have. Begin to take a mental inventory. If you want to take it to another level, write down all the things that you do have: a job, family, electricity, a car, etc. When you go back to being grateful about the things you have, you will learn to appreciate simple things more. You will also notice how people constantly talk about what they don't have. When you focus on what you don't have, you get more of what you don't have. When you are grateful for the things you do have, you will get more things. What I notice most commonly is that the people who don't have a lot are very grateful for what they do have. These people also take notice that many who have the most have no clue. Freedom to own a car, look at the Internet, or even vote are luxuries many would die to have and often sacrifice their lives to protect.

The final key to this *Tool* is that it is not just enough to acknowledge the things you have. That is the first step in using this *Tool*. The next part applies the ritual of giving thanks for what you have. Many ask, "Who do I give thanks to?" It can be God, a higher power or even the universe, it doesn't matter. Successful people know that this two-part ritual is key. Many of us did show gratitude in the form of prayer when we were kids. We knelt before our bed every night to pray and give thanks. Many families would say grace before dinner at night, giving thanks for the food they were about to eat.

We have gotten away from prayer and gratitude. These are just examples, you give thanks the way you feel appropriate and to whom you feel comfortable. When you do these two things — be thankful and give thanks — you will notice your level of happiness increases. You will notice that you have shifted your primary focus from lack to abundance, and in turn reap more abundance. When you use this *Tool*, you may feel a little silly that you didn't realize your good fortune — and others around you will also notice the change.

6. The five-minute rule.

We don't have a lot of time on this Earth. It is so important that we use all the strategies we can to keep our minds in good headspace. Don't waste brain power on particular things where you lack control. Depending upon who you are and your personal situation, many things occur that might make you mad. I mean we all have things that bother us now and then, and for the most part that is inevitable.

In the past when I'd get mad about something, it would consume me. I would spend a day or two steaming, talking about it to whoever would listen. When this happened, other aspects of my life suffered, including work, family and friends. They didn't do anything wrong so why should they have to suffer for something I felt worked up about? So, in turn, not only was I in a bad place inside my head, but the things in the world around me were negatively affected and responded accordingly.

Even if you are the type of person who keeps it "inside," those around you sense it. To prove it, when they feel it they say, "Is something wrong?" I don't even want to get into the health issues and physiological effects that anger has on a person. With regard to this book, we are talking about building success in your life — and anger does not play well with a happy, successful life. The truth is, you probably aren't mad enough to go to anger management. You just need a new *Tool* in your toolbox when the need arises.

You now have it, the five-minute rule. Warning, this *Tool* takes some practice to master. A rule I utilize when something disturbs me is to not let it bother me for more than five minutes. I look at my watch and stew about it for five minutes, then do my best to let it go. I know that in an hour or a day I will be over it, so why not shorten that time to five minutes and be done with it. This takes some practice and in the beginning will be hard to do. If you have something bugging you and the five-minute rule is not working, then use the 10-minute rule.

Here's the point, if you don't have a strategy to let go of your anger, you won't. In addition, when you let something keep you angry for a long period of time, they or it wins. Sometimes I found that I was angrier over being *angry!* I sometimes didn't even know why I was mad. As I began to work with this *Tool*, I was able to control anger.

Here is a bonus, when I really got good at this *Tool* I found that in general I was less angry and disturbed by things. Why? Because I made a mental choice that I didn't like the feeling of anger and I didn't like how it affected the things that mattered to me, including work, family and friends. When you get really good at this, you find others will get angry for you and sometimes mad that you aren't mad. Remember, angry people are not happy and part of a successful life is a happy one. So we must eliminate the things that hold us back — and anger is at the top of the list. We all know those people still angry over something that happened months or years ago — and a strong chance exists they won't experience a lot of growth and are probably in a pretty bad place. Use this *Tool* if anger holds you back from the success you desire and deserve.

7. Stop and smell the roses. OBG

If you are in the pursuit of happiness, it is wise to pause and be happy now and then. People like to say life is a marathon but they are wrong. Life is a series of sprints. In a marathon there are no breaks to stop and enjoy your work. Some driven, focused people miss some reached milestones. This *Tool* is as old as the early hammer. The concept has been around for ages and would be impossible to give any one person credit for coming up with it. Why has this *Tool*, like the hammer, lasted so long? It has a lot of value. Beauty and miracles surround you but you often fail to see them. You don't miss them because they are not there; you miss them because you fail to open your eyes and look.

When I began to use this *Tool*, I could not believe how much was going on around me. When I continued to push and reach new goals and new levels, I realized that the fulfillment that I used to get from reaching my goals was not there like it was before. I was reaching new levels and didn't even realize it. Before I even got a chance to celebrate my wins and achievements, I was setting new levels. Pushing harder and harder was not equating to being happier and happier. It was not computing in my brain as success. The simple reason was that I didn't stop to take a look around and realize how great things were around me right at that very moment.

Another thing happens when you stop and smell the roses around you, you slow down. You observe more and talk less; you listen more because you take in the surroundings. It is like a new level of consciousness that you have not felt for some time. Stop and celebrate your wins *(see Tool 24)*. You have roses all around you but if you don't stop to smell them, what good are they? Also, when you stop to smell the roses, you realize that most likely your life is right in the middle of a garden that not only has roses to smell but beautiful plants to observe.

When I started doing this *Tool*, I never realized how much beauty there was in the sky alone and it was free to look at. How many on their deathbed claim they wish they had taken more time to look around them? When you become an observer of life, you are more likely to have enjoyment in yours. You will be shocked at what you are missing around you simply because you never took the time to look.

8. Make a board of directors.

I love this one — and it is a great resource for solving problems. You will find this *Tool* in a book called *The Power of One* by Guy Reikman. Guy was the president of my college when I was going to school and has continued his work in the area of education. I saw him speak once, and he revealed a *Tool* that I had never heard of. He called it compiling a board of directors. If you do not have much experience in the corporate world, a board of directors is a group of usually 10 to 12 men and women who meet regularly to deal with company details and brainstorm on the company's problems and issues. This type of round table provides the benefit of more heads tackling a challenge. Quite often the people who sit on these boards bring their own education, backgrounds and experiences that strengthen the core's ability to come up with solid ideas to ensure success and avoid pitfalls and failures. As you begin to try and construct your successful life, you, too, will have problems arise that need advice and discussion. What if you had your own board?

Use this *Tool* to select 10 to 12 people who you would talk to if you needed advice on a particular issue. They can be anyone, alive or dead, if you know them or not. Pick the people you admire, a former president, philosopher, relative, anyone you would like to hear on a regular basis discuss challenges that come into your life. When you have put this list together, the next step is to put them all in a room at a desk and ask your question and then listen. Imagine how the conversation would go. What concerns would be brought up? What would be the reaction of those you have chosen for your board? At the end, if necessary, they can have a vote or ask you to provide them with new information. The possibilities are endless.

The component that makes this *Tool* unique is how you hear their opinions and advice. You may have limited access to some of the people you have chosen or they may no longer be alive. Also, this advice is not given one on one. It accounts for a large sample size of people whose opinion you respect and lets them come to a group conclusion or debate. You may not even get an answer; the group may be undecided. I believe such an imaginary forum will at worst give you perspectives you may have never considered or the ability to make a more informed decision on your question.

9. What would a Hall of Famer do?

To be recognized in any Hall of Fame means a person has achieved a level of excellence in his or her trade or profession. Those esteemed with the honor of being called a "Hall of Famer" have done so by applying strategies and illustrating characteristics that enable him or her to be acknowledged as the best of the best. Hall of Famers are blessed with particular gifts, but for the most part they have common traits that separate them from the rest. They have qualities, approaches and habits that distinguish them from others around them. Regardless of how they arrived at this level of excellence, I think we can all agree that incorporating the methods they use to achieve success in our own lives would be a definitive approach to emulate. Why reinvent what works? While the cliché, "Imitation is the sincerest form of flattery," is true, it also ensures the greatest probability of success.

This *Tool* becomes handy when you feel uncertain. Most of us fortunately know what a Hall of Famer would do. So if your goal is to be the best and reach levels you have never achieved before then ask yourself the question: What would a Hall of Famer do in this situation? A Hall of Famer doesn't make excuses. They accept responsibility for their actions. They never blame others. They do what others aren't willing to do.

What separates them from the average person? They willingly make that extra effort. A Hall of Famer possesses a burning desire to be his or her best. They understand that those who reach the top focus on what they want and where they want to go. They never take shortcuts and never cheat to get where they want to be. They understand that they would never sacrifice their principles to easily achieve something, which is never satisfying. They believe you must work for your goals.

Something you will discover in *Tool 97, You will always remember what came hard and mostly forget what came easy.* Understand that to be a Hall of Famer is not only a recognized achievement. One can reach this status by being a great parent, friend or mentor. So if you struggle on what it takes to reach the level of success you hope to achieve then ask yourself, "What would a Hall of Famer do?" Approaching your life in this fashion will drastically increase the likelihood of reaching your goals and avoiding the pitfalls that have sabotaged your dreams.

10. Get up earlier.

There are so many reasons for adding this *Tool* to your arsenal. Getting up earlier in the morning assists you in so many challenges you may be having. Early rising tackles the complaint about lack of time. If you only got up one hour earlier a day, that would give you a whole extra day's worth of time every month. The truth really is not that you don't have enough time but that you don't have enough energy.

We covered a little bit about what causes us to be low on our energy level, which is nutrition and exercise, but with regard to getting up earlier — we oversleep.

I find most people say they need 7-8 hours of sleep but they *don't* sleep for all that time. When I started getting up at 5:00 a.m. every morning, it was hard at first. Then I started to get used to it and I liked it. When others found out I did this, they assumed I had to go to bed at 9:00 p.m. every night. The truth was I went to bed around 11:00 p.m. but I slept for a solid six hours. You see, it is not totally about the number of hours but the quality of sleep in those hours. This will vary from person to person, but you can get by on less sleep if it is *quality* sleep.

Some of the other advantages of getting up earlier are getting a workout in and sitting down to a good, hot breakfast. If you feel constantly late or hate traffic, early rising remedies those problems. Finally, you will feel great peace of mind at the end of the day that you completed a number of tasks in the morning, which frees you up for activities at night. By applying this simple *Tool*, you will get more done, be in less of a rush, and get the best quality sleep you've ever had.

11. Smile first and see the reaction you get from others.

This is actually a fun one to try, and my self-kept statistics have it working about 90 percent of the time. The concept is simple, before you walk up to any person or into any situation put on a smile. Nine times out of 10 the person will smile back and that sets up the interaction to have a greater probability of success or positive interaction. You will benefit by drastically reducing the probability of rejection. Without talking you disarm the person, who is now much more receptive to your communication. The person you interact with has received few smiles or compliments all day. The possibility exists that you may even be the first to do so.

The second part of this strategy sets up a more enjoyable interaction. Human nature suggests that people will be more cooperative when they deal with someone they like. So you have a small window of opportunity to be liked, especially if you deal with someone at a counter who has been getting yelled at all day. When you come up with your smile on, you've created a "timeout" for them.

In my travels I have had to deal with a flight agent or two. These people get yelled at more for no reason than in other industries. Walking up to these people with a smile on my face has helped me get where I was going more often than not. I am convinced I have made flights, connections, and received better seating because of a simple smile. If you asked service people, or any who work in other industry for that matter, I bet they would tell you when they can that they will go out of their way for someone who has a smile on their face.

I'm also certain that if I asked you to think of the people you know who always have a smile on their face, you could name them. Chances are you have a smile on your face just thinking about that person or persons. The truth is if you smile at someone, they almost have to try not to smile back. And when you get a smile on someone's face, they are much more likely to cooperate with you and assist you the best they can. Keep in mind I am not saying to use this to get your way, people can see through that insincerity right away; but when you put a routine smile into practice, it becomes automatic. And you become one of those people who smiles all the time.

12. You never get a second chance at a first impression. OBG

When something provides value, it possesses the ability to stand the test of time. This is no different when making a first impression. Why do first impressions play an integral role in fostering success? Because once someone has their mind set, it becomes difficult to change it. When a person forms that first impression, they label that person — and labels are hard to change. Have you ever heard of "self-fulfilling prophecy?" Self-fulfilling prophecy suggests that the person holds a belief about another person's skills, abilities or characteristics. So if I think someone is always late, any time they are late reinforces my belief about that person. Even if the person really is habitually late, since I have labeled them as a "late person," they never get credit for being on time but only further my belief every time they are late.

Coaches are often cautioned on doing the same thing. If they think a player is good, they will spend extra time assisting them to improve their game, and in turn, they get even better. If they are just happy when a kid "tries hard," they say, "Nice job, Johnny," and send him back to the end of the line. Are you beginning to see how first impressions can cause an implant into someone's brain? I am not saying it is right to judge people in this manner; but most people's brains are wired this way — and by knowing this, you may need to use this *Tool* to accomplish some goals and successes that you have had difficulty reaching.

"Well, I should be able to be how I want to be or wear what I want to wear." You're correct, you do have that right, but you may have to lower some expectations. Let me give you an example. I knew a young professional who was very bright and had a lot going for him. While he was in graduate school, he used to dress like a punk rocker. He had a very difficult time getting people to take him seriously. In addition, jobs and internships were hard to come by because, even when cleaned up, you could still tell that something wasn't right. Even when wearing a suit, he had a way of assigning a punk twist to it and little could be done to make colored hair look right. This young man had a lot to say and many things that he hoped to accomplish. To reach these aspirations, he needed a platform and an arena to do so. What did he do? He toned down his image. He realized that while he had things that he wanted to do and say, the possibility of reaching his goals would increase if he could reach more people and find more open doors of opportunity. So he made this a reality by not changing who he was but conforming a bit to what the general public was comfortable with.

Now I am not telling you to march like a good drummer boy or girl and be what others want you to be. But people's image or first impression of you will open more opportunities. If you decide you are not willing to change to reach your goals be willing to accept that it may be harder to reach to achieve those goals. Think of your first impression with someone as planting a seed. If the seed you plant will grow weeds, don't be surprised when you don't get an apple tree. If you plant a positive image from the start, you will have little hedge work to perform later.

13. Readers are leaders, one book a week.

When I finally finished with graduate school I made one promise, it was to never read another book again. Big mistake. I only made the problem worse by telling myself that I had no time to read. Then I came up with the excuse that I had four or five trade magazines to read each month and that was all the reading I could fit in. These trade magazines were important and would keep me up-to-date on things in my profession, things that I could apply to help with patients. However, I have never used one thing I have read in a trade magazine to improve patient care. One reason is that I was never really reading them. Instead I was skimming them to see if there were any articles that looked worth reading. I would also look at the ads and the pictures to see if anything caught my eye. The truth was that I barely read them and when I did, they provided little benefit. The other excuse that I did not have time to read was untrue; I simply chose to do other things with my time than read. When I began to read, my life improved 50 percent right on the spot. It did so twofold. First, it was the type of books I chose to read; and second, it was shedding activities I was doing when I wasn't reading.

Let's start with the choice of books you make. Remember, our brain is a computer so we should be very careful what we decide to put into it. The same goes for reading books. I believe you choose books that will improve your life, and in turn, the lives of the people around you. I choose to read the so-called "self-help" books. Knowing that the better place I'm in improves the environment around me, why wouldn't I read helpful books? These books provide so many diamonds for you to use and apply and share. This is exactly what I am doing with you.

The problem is not that you can't handle the job; the problem is you don't have the *Tools* or instructions for the job. I try to take two to three things out of all the books I read. You are not going to do everything a book suggests, but by incorporating a few things you will be helped on your path to success. Just like you should stay away from the newspaper and tabloids, stay away from garbage books as well. Choose not to put garbage into your computer.

A strategy for reading that my mentor taught me was to read a book once. Then read it a second time and highlight important parts. Then read it one last time and take notes. By doing so, you have turned the book into a quick reference guide that you can go back to over and over. It can take a long time trying to find something that you read in a book some time ago. Remind yourself you are trying to do the things that the most successful people are doing — and this is definitely one of them. Read enough good stuff and you will be writing your book to help others in your own special way.

Remember I also mentioned reading helps you stay away from things that don't particularly foster success; things like texting, talking on the phone, playing on the Internet, video games, too much TV, and so on and so on. You know the things that you do during the day that provide little progress toward reaching your goals and assisting the overall plan of success.

I like to read before I go to bed. That way information stays with me right before I sleep and it actually helps me fall asleep. The more *good* books you read, the more you will want to read. You will find that the distractions and excuses you used to not read will become less appealing. You will find that you will be able to help more people as your headspace starts to grow. Also, if you try to give someone a book to help them and they choose not to read it, well, you have done your best to help out. You can't make them grab the life preserver. A large portion of where I am today is because I decided to read more, read well and by doing so rid myself of distractions that held me back from where I wanted to go.

14. Pray.

To make this easy to implement daily, do it at your bedside before you go to bed. I remember this being a habit that I used to do with my parents as a child — and you can do with your child if you like. Even saying thanks at dinner as a family is a form of prayer. Prayer keeps us in the habit of being thankful for what we have and focused on thinking about others. Prayer also does not have to be just about God. It can be Buddha, a higher power, or simply *Tool 5*, which is *Be grateful for the things you have and give thanks*. Soon you will read *Tool 67*, which is *Compile a team of experts*. My expert in this department is Pastor Steve Curran, and I asked him to contribute to the *Tool* by sharing what prayer is. I think sometimes the reason we don't pray is because we are not sure how.

Prayer is intimate communication between God and a person. As in any loving relationship, communication involves active listening and verbalizing. We all have experienced good, bad and indifferent communication with other people. We know that the best communication happens when people talking with each other are involved and interested in the welfare of the other — heart, mind, and soul. Prayer at its best is just like that.

One simple way to grow in your prayer experience with God is to use an "A.C.T.S." method in a specific time of focused prayer. This time can be short or long, but it is focused loving communication between you and God. Begin in a quiet place free of distractions. Place yourself in a position that helps you comfortably focus on being attentive to God. Begin your time of prayer with ADORATION.

Adore God for who He is. Praise God for all that you have experienced with Him; all of His beauty and strength and holy transcendence that you have experienced in ways large or small. Focus on the ways that God has revealed His glory to you, and express to Him your heart's response.

Next, CONFESS: name and admit your errors, mistakes, faults, and ways you have harmed yourself, others, or your relationship with God. The purpose is not to be morbidly self focused, but to keep one's relationship with God, the lover of your soul, free of anything that would inhibit the free flow of love between God and you. Confession removes any little pebbles in your shoe, so you may walk closely with God throughout your day.

THANKFULNESS flows naturally after confession. God's love for you is new every morning. Great is His faithfulness to love and forgive and restore and heal. Think and remember all the good things He has done in your life. Remember answers to prayer requests you have made. Be specific in your gratitude for all the goodness He has shown you.

Lastly, conclude with SUPPLICATION. Make your needs and requests known to God. Ask for what you need. Make requests on behalf of others. Ask for God's intervention, grace, help, healing, mercy, strength, love, or anything else that is in your heart. Whatever you ask, believe that He hears you, and that it is His delight to answer the prayers of all who seek Him in earnest humility and dependence on His grace. Trust in His love and wisdom and guidance in your relationship.

There are many facets to prayer. The A.C.T.S. method is only one small one. One book you might explore to continue your growth in prayer is from the Northumbria Community, *The Celtic Book of Daily Prayer.*

15. Pick a charity.

I have noticed lack of purpose in life prevents some people from achieving personal growth and achieving success in their lives. They often feel little need or desire to work on themselves. They may feel they live mundane lives and see small benefit to strive to reach their dreams. I believe when you focus on something larger than yourself, it rejuvenates you. This is how finding a charity to support can be a wonderful *Tool* to help realign your priorities to work on areas of your own life.

The first part of this *Tool* that helps you work your blueprint is seeing people who are often less fortunate than you. By helping others overcome their challenges in life, you begin to wonder what your excuse is. Why are you not doing the best you can do with the obstacles you need to overcome? You may also discover some methods and insights on how people with difficulties handle those issues. The more you see people strive to survive and succeed, the more likely you will do the same.

Next, feeling needed by a charitable organization and the people benefiting from the generosity of that charity gives you a sense of belonging, a sense of being a part of something larger than yourself. This feeling will spark a need for self improvement. You feel needed, which puts you in a better place and more apt to help others. In addition, you will seek out new information to help those in need that by nature will only rub off on yourself as you strive for success. Not to mention the constant thank you's that you will receive — that alone will make you feel better about yourself. There is no greater reward than helping others.

By entering a new arena that you know little about and them knowing little about you, provides an opportunity for personal reinvention. People are always asking for a fresh start. Well, here is your chance. If you are always late, start arriving early to your new charity. If you feel you need to be more of a leader, there are plenty of opportunities in charitable organizations for leadership positions. Any area that you want to start becoming better at you can. These new people will only know you based on your performance within the organization. You have the opportunity to be however you want to be.

Lastly, if every one of us picked our own charitable organization, could you imagine how much better the world would be? We are not just talking about donating money. Often your time is far more important to a group than just cash. The impact would be widely felt; smaller government, smaller taxes and the ability to help others out of a sense of duty, not obligation. If everyone picked a charity of their own, the world would be a much happier place.

16. Make a dream board.

Until I watched the video of *The Secret*, I had never heard of this before. I have to believe that many have heard about it by now. A dream board is a large piece of construction paper where you cut out things that you would like to have and paste them onto the board. The belief is that by doing this action, it increases the possibility you will acquire these things or things like them. What is pretty incredible is this worked all too well for the gentleman in *The Secret*. While moving into a new house and unpacking his things, he discovered that a house he had put on an old dream board of his was the house he was moving into now. What are the chances? I am not a statistician, but I don't need a degree in statistics to know they are incredibly low.

Why does a dream board work? Well, the stance of those in *The Secret* is that you ask the universe for something and it grants your request. I can handle that, but just for argument's sake, let's say that is too much for you to chew. I believe the take-home message: Keep your eye on the prize. Attain things you desire and strive for keep you on track to do the things you need to do to accomplish your goals.

We are not just talking about material things. If you just want happiness for you and those around you, you may paste images of people smiling on your dream board. If your goal is to get into shape, you may put pictures up of healthy-looking people. I would even put up pictures of yourself when you believed you looked good. This is just another *Tool* whereby I believe the "action" of what you do makes it work for you. These boards can be thought of as mini bulls' eyes that keep you focused and give you targets to shoot for. Thinking you want a nice car someday versus taking the time to cut one out, paste it to a board, and then place that board up somewhere are very different. Just like writing things down on your blueprint sheet, this is a way of writing down "images" of success and "images" of what you want. Now go get your scissors and glue and start dream boarding.

17. Become a better listener.

God gave you two ears and one mouth for a reason, so you listen twice as much as you speak. I actually hated it when adults used to say that to me, even though it is a very good premise to live by. I believe this is one of the most difficult *Tools* to use and to get good at. It takes some practice, but if you walked into a hardware store, not everything is as simple as a screwdriver — some tools require training and time to become good at using them.

When I listened more I benefited by getting more from the conversation. For example, when I interrupted with a question, the person was getting to that answer if I had let them finish. Allowing the person to talk and finish what they have to say cuts my talk time almost in half. When you interrupt or ask questions in the middle of someone talking, it is not only rude but it can also take the conversation in a different direction when it may have gone where you wanted to go all along.

One time I was talking with someone and made an extra effort to let them talk out their point. I did this so well that the person said hello on the phone because they weren't sure if I was still there. I also like it because it allows you to talk and make your point uninterrupted. When someone does interrupt you, you can ask them, "Didn't I let you have your say?" The person then has two options. They can either let you finish or interrupt. If they let you finish, great. If they keep interrupting you, then you can feel no regret in cutting the conversation short and know you did your best.

Better listening also benefits from human nature — the fact is people like talking about themselves. So when you let them do this, you boost and stroke their egos by simply shutting up. When you are the type of person who listens and makes people feel better about themselves just by listening to them, you increase success probabilities. People will like you more and be more apt to help you accomplish your goals because you make them feel good about themselves.

Finally, this may be a good *Tool* to use if you just simply won't shut up. You may, on the other hand, close many avenues or shut out people who can help you reach goals because you never listen to anything they say. If you become the person who never listens to what anyone says or who never takes advice (especially when you ask for it), people are just going to stop bothering. You know who these people are and you know if you are one of them.

I see this as a very low-risk *Tool* to incorporate. What do you have to lose? By listening more than you speak, you gather more information, can often make people more comfortable around you, and lastly have the chance of to make people feel better because you allowed them to talk about their favorite topic, *them*. This is a sneaky little *Tool* because it doesn't require that you do more, it requires that you do less. Just remember, this one takes some practice to master and there are not many out there who have.

18. Turn off the TV.

Do I really even have to write anything here? With the amount of TV people watch, I am guessing that I do. Here is one reason to keep reading and considering this *Tool*. First, are you someone who says, "I just don't have enough time?" Second, do you watch TV? Enough said. In a recent study by Nielson, a person watches an estimated four hours and 45 minutes per day. *Are you kidding me!?* These figures were accumulated over the 2007-2008 season. Is it any wonder why we are fatter than we have ever been? Is it any wonder why we are sadder than we have ever been? Is it any wonder why we are sicker than we have ever been? To make it worse, you watch these shows and news broadcasts that tell you how bad things are and then the commercials tell you what drugs to take to make it all better. I saw a commercial for restless leg syndrome and thought it was a TV skit. Right now they are working on a drug for shyness in children. I digress. Remember, your brain is nothing more than a computer and whatever you decide to put into it is what will end up eventually coming out of it.

There are so many unnecessary things we watch on TV. The news would be a prime suspect. Is there anything on the news that you have heard that you *really* need to know. People are shot; there is a fire in your town; it's going to be 64 degrees tomorrow. Do you really need to hear this over and over again? I promise you if there is something newsworthy that you need to know, someone will end up telling you about it. Use others as your filter for what you decide to hear every day. If something really bad happens, someone will bring it up or call you. When I stopped watching the news, I have not missed anything that I am aware of, and when there has been something semi-big, a friend or patient will say, "Hey did you hear about …?" Even when they do that, I choose not to listen half the time because I don't want that junk in my head.

What's really big right now is reality TV, which by all accounts is not even really that real. How do I know? Because I was on a reality show once and from what I could tell, only about 20-30 percent was real. Don't believe me? Well, on this one show the director asked us to stop because it was boring and no one cared and we needed to start the "reality" scene again. Why would you ever want to watch people fighting with each other or watch the drama that is occurring in someone else's house or life. Do you not have enough things to worry about on your own? When I decided to turn my TV off for a whole month, I found that I was almost bored. I had to find things to do with the added time I had. I worked out, I read, and I did house projects that had sat there because there was no time to do them. I started working on the things in my life and not watching other people's lives on the magic box.

Almost five hours a day of TV is 35 hours a week. If you only decided to watch half the TV that you watch, you would have at least an extra 15 hours a week. I think with that time you could find some time to work out and read. Those two things alone would improve your life by 50 percent. Watch half the TV you watch and use the other time to work out four to five days a week and read one book per week.

Now does this mean that you should get rid of your television? Of course not. How would you see me touring the country talking about my book? I'm just kidding. By knowing what the national average is, be aware of how much you watch and if you claim not to have enough time. I think informative programs, historical programs and sports are acceptable. Those programs either provide you information or, with regard to sports shows (for the most part), celebrate people's wins. It's beneficial to watch an athlete who sets goals and then achieves them. If you struggle with time or just need to get off the couch, use this *Tool* to take you to the next level.

19. Positive thinking always works better than negative thinking.

You may find confronting your thoughts the most difficult thing in the world; but it is also one of the most important things you need to address on your journey toward a better life. The way you think has multiple levels of how it affects the success you reach in your life. Although I think most of us know this and I doubt very many would argue about it, I think the key to using this *Tool* is as a reminder.

No one likes to be around "Debbie Downer" or "Don Depressing." Once again, you know this person in your life and once again, it might be you. Let's analyze why people think negatively. It is often easier to be negative than to be positive. Think about it. If you're negative and something bad happens, you were right. If you are negative and something good happens, then it almost works out as a nice surprise. I think many are afraid to use positive thinking and then not receive the result they expected. It sets you up for others to break you down for thinking positive and having a setback.

The truth is we deal with percentages. Those who think positively have a greater percentage of success and achieved goals. These are also the people we call "lucky." They seem to have things work out their way most of the time, while those who think negatively ultimately get their wish. Then to make it worse, when they do have some achievement in their life, they are less likely to appreciate it. In addition, these people dislike positive-thinking people. And most likely positive-thinking people don't really like being around them either. Positive thinking comes with a risk that you must be willing to accept. When you have a setback, many will criticize you for the way you think and will say that thinking positively only sets you up for being disappointed and it's unrealistic. For your information, the most successful people in the world became that way by being "unrealistic."

If you need something more scientific to help you believe, let's talk physiology. It has become well-accepted and is no surprise that your body's chemical makeup and body language change with how you think. I once heard that more heart attacks occur on Monday than any other day. Gee, I wonder what most people's thoughts are on a Monday. Another aspect is body language. We all know that people can pick up on our body language. When you are a negative thinker, what do you think your expressions look like? How does a negative person think and breathe? When someone is negative, they just look and act different. Lastly, people don't want to be around negative thinkers. Therefore, positive, successful people are going to do little to go out of their way to help a negative person. They are going to do little to foster a negative person's success or help them reach their goals. Negative thinkers generally hang around other negative thinkers. This is one double negative that does not make a positive. If you are still struggling with negative thinking, read *The Power of Positive Thinking* by Norman Vincent Peale. This book is an instruction book on how to help you master this *Tool*. Light will always illuminate the dark, but dark will never shut out the light.

20. Connect the rings.

It's not about meeting the right person; it's about being the right person. I have added this *Tool* to the box to help you if you are having relationship challenges and to strengthen your will to work on who you are. In the movie, *Jerry Maguire*, Tom Cruise comes home to tell his wife, "You complete me." The thought in the scene being that without her, he is not whole. In other words, what many of us want is to be "needed" by someone else, because if the person we are with "needs" us, they are less likely to leave. In addition, if they need us badly enough, we can get away with things because there is little risk of being left or facing consequences for our actions because we need each other to make one whole.

Well, I am here to tell you Cruise was wrong. The statement should have been, "You complement me." Not very romantic, I know. You shouldn't be looking for someone to complete you; you should be looking to complete yourself. Herein lies the problem, we spend all this time looking for the perfect person rather than trying to become that perfect person, a *Tool* developed from my reading of *The Celestine Prophecy* by James Redfield.

If you look at a relationship as a ring, when you complete someone, you are part of the ring and they are the other part. That is how the connection is made. It is based on the need for one another to make something whole. Let me show you another way. If two people work on making themselves one complete ring, then they can align themselves with others and make a chain of interconnected, but separate rings. The beauty of the chain creates a strong bond where each ring complements each other and works together to build overall strength. So each complete ring does not require the other to complete itself. Now in all honesty, our rings are never totally complete because we always work on making ourselves complete. Looking at the first model, those don't resemble rings but C's or a half-eaten doughnut, and that leaves too much room for self-improvement.

The flow of needing someone to complete you means their strengths are your weaknesses, which gives you little incentive to work on these areas because you don't have to. Don't misunderstand what I am saying. I truly believe that a couple is a team, and teammates help each other to succeed in areas where they need help, but they do so by raising the other one up to success. Also, if something does happen years later and we lose the other half of our completed ring, we feel lost. We have done little to improve our weak spots. Now we are thrown right into the fire to try to improve them. Most often improving these areas takes time and we do not respond well to this immediate need. We all have important strengths. We will have stronger and weaker portions of our ring. Yet when we expect "completion" we risk weaknesses in those areas.

This is why I believe the statistics are higher for divorce if you are married before 30. Before we reach 30, we barely have rings to connect with someone else. On or around this time, we possess the ability to make a chain with another person but continue to work on our own. A great union can be built by two people who connect, maintain their identities, and support each one's direction. Two rings connected in this way put those two people together on a journey. Your bond grows and becomes stronger and makes your *individual* ring more resilient.

By continually working on yourself you grow together. Best of all, when you celebrate what you like most about the other, you help their ring become stronger, as opposed to always harping on their shortcomings, which in turn, weakens that part of their ring. Don't get caught being weak and looking for someone to make you whole. Don't look outside yourself for happiness and success. Focus on being the right person and when you find someone else who has done the same, you will connect the rings and form a strong bond that complements, not one that completes.

21. Life is like a game, there are different ways to play but you play to win.

Why would you play it any other way? And here's another thing, you are playing right now whether you like it not. Your objective must be to win. This mentality needs to be established before you even hit the field. Let's say for example there were only three options. You had a choice to not care, survive or win the game. That leaves you with three directions, two of which will not lead to success. So by choosing to win, you increase your probability of success by eliminating the two choices that almost ensure that you won't win. If your daily mantra is to simply make it through the day, you will do just that; but if each day your mantra involves making the most of the day, seizing opportunities, taking all actions to win, and making decisions to go for it, you will be tuned in on that expectation. Not to mention the subconscious programming that occurs from this line of thinking. If you just try to survive the day, you will tread water enough to barely keep your head above it. Decide to win and increase your probability of rising above.

To win the game you need to know the rules of how to win. If you don't know the rules before you play, you have no chance. Those reaching the levels of success understand the rules and what needs to be done to win. When I say win, I mean achieve success, and let me remind you, you determine what success means to you. You decide what winning the game requires. The rules are those things at your disposal to get you to where you want to go. These are all the things we have discussed earlier — knowing who you are (mission statement); where you want to go (goals); and how to build toward that (*Tools*).

Games become much easier when you know the tricks on how to succeed. When you hold the ball or joystick, remember that you make choices of what to do with it. I can promise you this, when you aren't focused on what to do with it, you severely limit your ability to come out on top. When you make the decision to win, all your energy becomes focused in that direction. When all your efforts are focused in one direction, you increase the probability of heading in that direction. That direction is: *To win the game*.

22. There is only one group of people who don't have problems, dead people.

We all have challenges, so when it seems like you are the only one having challenges, take solace in knowing you're not. Challenges are a part of life and how we deal with them is what makes a great life. When you get to *Tool 62*, you will see that happy people work on solutions, unhappy people talk about problems. For now, understand that we all have things that we deal with. I found this *Tool* so helpful for so many reasons. I used to think that successful people don't have the problems that I have. I used to think that those who do have problems didn't have problems like mine. I also used to use the problems I had as excuses and crutches for the reasons I was being held back. The strength of this *Tool* is perspective.

The first mistake we make is in thinking that those who are successful don't have problems. *They do.* Successful people have the same problems we all do. The reason why this isn't evident to you and me is twofold. They don't work on the problems, they focus on solutions. They also turn problems into challenges. We all dwell on problems and let them hold us down. By flipping them to challenges, successful people focus on strategies to fix them. Knowing there is a difference allows you to separate the two. A perfect example, think of all the people you know who have "problems." They make for an easy excuse and only take us in one direction; but when we change these problems to challenges, we open ourselves up to an action plan for solutions.

We also often fall into believing our problems are worse than other people's problems. *They aren't.* All problems we face seem large — larger to us because we feel forced to deal with them. When we make problems larger than other people's problems, it gives us an "out" to make them harder to deal with. It gives us the ability to fail because others don't deal with what we deal with. All challenges are large to us because they are *our* challenges. What determines the size of the fire is our ability to put it out. Meaning, if you don't know how to tackle a problem, you won't. The ability to deal with challenges determines the size of the problem. Hopefully the skills and systems we put in place right now will provide you with the ability to make these problems workable. Losing the perception that your problems are bigger than everyone else's gives you resolve to conquer these challenges.

The bottom line: We all have to deal with things. What is the difference? Successful people don't have your problems because they know how to deal with them. Remember this book's affirmation, *"The road to success is always under construction."* The belief that you will be on cruise control at any point in your life will never happen. You will constantly work to reach new levels of success — and to do this means that you will have to deal with roadblocks that appear along the way. When you accept that we all have a full cup to manage the excuse factor disappears. You erase the notion that luckiness or easiness exists for one person and not for you. If you feel you have few problems, realize everyone has challenges and struggles — then realize successful people understand how to manage them.

23. If I talked to you the way you talked to yourself, you'd hate me.

How many times have you said, "I'm dumb" or "I'm an idiot?" When you say it enough times, the brain starts to believe it. Negative self talk plays an integral role in self perception. The brain cannot tell the difference between a real event versus one thought up in the mind. Let me give you an example. They asked one group of people to practice shooting free throws each day. Then they asked a second group of people to just visualize in their minds that they were shooting free throws. The third group they asked to do nothing. What they found is when they tested their free-throwing ability later, the group that practiced in their minds did just about as well as the group that actually went out and practiced. The mind processed the information in the same way. The brain does the same thing with what we tell it over and over and over.

Now even I will catch myself saying what an idiot I am when I screw up on something. It is human nature to be our own worst critic. The key is twofold. First, be aware of your self-talk and make a conscious effort to not say negative things to yourself. Instead of saying, "I'm an idiot," I like to replace it with, "That's not like me." I also find by knowing that how I talk to myself forms my brain's perception of who I am, I now compliment myself more. When I do something right or kind, I let myself know it. If I hold a door open for someone, I will tell myself, "Nice job buddy." I find when I do that, not only does the act of doing something nice for someone else feel good, but the pat I give myself on the back makes me want to have that feeling more often. Finally, when I do say something negative to myself, I quickly say, "I didn't mean that," or as a mentor of mine used to simply say, "Delete." He even said it out loud. I have found you can do this for anything you don't want to put in your head.

It will feel weird in the beginning. If this is new to you, of course, it's going to feel a little strange. But as with any new skill, it takes practice. As you start to practice doing this, it becomes automatic. You should see the look on people's faces when I make the statement, "If I talked to you the way you talk to yourself, you would hate me." People can really identify with the statement because we all do it. If you do the negative talk enough, your brain and body start to believe it. So let's use this powerful *Tool* to our advantage and program our brains to work for us and roadblock the junk we want to keep out.

24. Review the wins you have each week.

As we play the game of life, we will have wins and losses. We must first accept that both exist and will occur. You will have things you did right and things you did wrong. What we are trying to do during the game is to have more wins than losses. In using this logic, we think of wins and losses as two sides to a scale or a balance sheet. This thinking is flawed when evaluating success. This *Tool* works by giving added weight to wins and devaluating losses to the realm of redirection. For the sake of this *Tool*, let's simply say each win is a step forward and each loss is a step sideways. What I want you to do is look at wins as positive and losses as neutral. Now I understand that some losses can be bigger than others. I also understand some major losses can be larger setbacks in our crusade toward success. For now just humor me in my endeavor to make a point. The point, you are doing a lot right and you don't even know it.

For many of you this should be one of the first *Tools* you choose to install in your blueprint. Reason, identifying wins accomplishes many things. The first being you may not even realize that you are doing things right. When we focus on all the shortcomings we have, we only work on shortcomings. When we accentuate and celebrate the things we do right, we strengthen those things that work. We need to give more power to wins and use losses as ways to refocus. You first need to know you can run to know you can run a mile. In the same respect, you need to see that you are doing things right to know you can do other things right. The only way you can know this is to celebrate the "right."

This *Tool* forces you to change your assessment of how the week went; meaning instead of dwelling on negatives, celebrate positives. You will find this hard to do at first. The negatives are easy because they cause pain, and we have come to accept them and expect them. We need to retrain our mind to look for wins and expect them to happen. By doing so, we open the door for more wins and allow them to happen. Also, when we identify wins for the week, we increase the probability they will continue, thus increasing the likelihood of them becoming habit. List all the wins you have each week. Don't worry about how big, small or obscure. Enforce the direction of wins and successes. By doing more to pave the road toward success you open the door for additional achievements. Knowing you can accomplish will allow you to *accomplish*.

25. Don't let your music die inside of you. What music do you have to play?

I hope you find a *Tool* that has the same influence that this *Tool* had on me. I had received an email about Wayne Dyer coming to speak at a college right down the road. I honestly didn't recognize his name. I was drawn by the subject he was going to discuss and that the cost was only $50. As I remember, I had many excuses not to go. Using one of the *Tools* that I will share with you (*46, The best investment you will ever make is in your mind*), I attended the event. He had a lot of great information that he shared that night. When I hear a speaker or read a book, my goal is to come away with one thing that I can apply in my life. *Tool 25* is what pushed this book into reality.

Dyer spoke of a fable about a man who was unhappy with everything about his life. This man went back and forth to work, missing everything all around him and cursing all that was his life. In the end on his deathbed, he ponders the question of if he did it right. The man was contemplating what he had made of his life. I am doing little justice to the story and apparently it's one that many have heard; but what I heard next was something I had never thought about. Dyer said, "Don't let your music die inside of you. What music do you have to play?" That was the day I knew I had to write this book.

What he was trying to say was that we all have something to say, something to contribute. If we don't do it now, we may end up on our deathbed full of regret. Now I don't think it has to be that extreme. What I do believe about this *Tool* is that we need to make it happen now. Believe that you are not insignificant and that your ideas have value and need to be expressed. When I first heard this, I was thinking about how I better do this book before something happens to me. Later, I realized the message went deeper. The more important message suggests we all have music to play. We all have an instrument in the band that we play. By not letting your music die inside of you, you grow not only yourself, but the harmony of the band.

26. Effective leaders lead by example.

If you remember, in Chapter 1 I mentioned that I was struggling with issues in my practice. This is a perfect example of a *Tool* I learned that helped with one particular challenge I was having. As an employer I expected my employees to be on time. Now my definition of on time was not one to two minutes before your shift started. I expected you to be ready for work a few minutes prior so when patients first arrive, they can have your full attention. The problem was this occurred rarely if at all. Often patients would be waiting for the door to open, or if the front door was unlocked, they walked into an office that was not ready to begin operation.

When I discussed this with my employees, they had excuses of traffic and other issues. Soon after we would discuss it, they would be on time for a few days and then they seemed to fall back into their old habits. Now many would say, "Why didn't you just fire them?" Trust me; it is much easier to train someone than to find someone. So what I did at the time was what a nail would do, blame the problem on everything else. Blame it on the fact that employees just don't listen and don't care. Blame the world that they just didn't make them like they used to. Then something happened. I realized that when you point your finger at someone else, there are three pointing right back at yourself. There was the problem. Guess who was coming to work one minute before he was supposed to see patients? Guess who was late some days when he was supposed to see patients? Bingo, it was me. So once I learned this *Tool*, which I had heard many times before but never learned, things began to change. I made a decision at that point that not only would I be the first to arrive at my office, I would have *everything* up and running before the first person arrived, employee or patient. Then you'll never guess what started to happen. My employees started arriving on time. In fact, my present office manager beats me to the office most days by a half hour before her shift.

There is a key to properly using this *Tool*. This one only works if done consistently, and by that I mean 99 percent of the time — that is what leading by example means; doing things consistently at the highest level so much so that it makes others want to strive for that level as well. People are more likely to do things you ask of them if they see you walking your talk. They are also more likely to do what their leader is doing because they don't feel like they are the only ones doing it. People by nature want to be part of a team and if they see the team captain doing it, they believe it is what is expected by other teammates to be part of the team. You foster an environment that makes people want to be better because you don't direct people, you lead them. People will be led to do anything if they believe in their leader. I can't think of a better way to have people believe in you than by doing what you say is important.

27. Surround yourself with growth-oriented people.

There are two types of people, motors and anchors. Motors are going somewhere, anchors just drag you down. In the beginning of the book, we expressed this view on how there are two types of people in this world. I find that the successes of many are not solely held back by themselves but by the company they keep.

This does not mean blaming others for holding you back. What it means is your surroundings affect your ability to achieve happiness.

For example, think about a garden. If you try to grow a specific vegetable or flower, you can't just throw some seeds on the ground. You need to surround it with soil that gives it the best chance to thrive. You need to remove weeds that cause problems. You also need to work it with water and fertilizer, and on occasion do a little bug removal. What this all means is that you choose where to plant your seeds and what things will surround your garden.

This can be a hard *Tool* to use. Family members and long-time friends often surround us. Herein lies the question, do you continue to hang out with these people knowing they sidetrack you along this journey of life? If you have trouble *growing*, take a look around you. Growth in a toxic environment can be difficult. You may find it hard to build anything when you must constantly repair things.

28. Eat with your head days one through six, eat with your heart on day seven.

There are things we love to eat and then there are things we know we should eat. Unfortunately for most of us, the things we love to eat are bad for us and the things we know we should eat aren't at the top of our list. If you need a *Tool* to help you with the Nutrition section of your form, try this. Look at your week and find six days to eat the way you know you should. This will differ from person to person depending upon nutritional goals and needs. Then identify one day that you can eat whatever you like. I find Sunday as a free day works best for me; but I also change that day when I see something coming up that could cause trouble. If I'm going to the California State Fair on a Friday night, I know the *hazards* that will be there in every food court so I change that to my free day.

This technique works well because it makes it easy to be aware of what you should be eating that day and avoid cheating. It also helps you avoid being bad by knowing you have a reward day coming up. I also like this approach, because if I ate well all week I didn't want to eat that much garbage on my free day. So I ended up not really pigging out like the free day would imply. This *Tool* really illustrates a perfect example of how the book's system works. In the Nutritional section of

SANE, you enter your goals for your nutritional intake. Then in the *Tool* section, you pick something like this to help implement it and make the goal become reality. So give it a try if this is an area of struggle for you and see if it helps out.

29. 211 vs. 212

I have to give credit to www.simpletruths.com for this *Tool*. As you strive to learn more on how to succeed and improve your outlook on life, I believe they are tops in this department. I was lucky enough to see this video called *212, The Extra Degree* at a seminar and it really made a lot of sense. You see, at 211 degrees water is very, very hot, but at 212 degrees water is boiling and begins to produce steam. This lesson in science teaches us something just as important in life. It shows us that with just a little more effort makes a significant difference and change in something. Many of us don't tackle personal goals and growth, because we mistakenly believe it's too hard and requires too much effort. If we understand this principle then we know a small amount of additional effort takes our situation from not just good but great.

I think what can also be taken away from knowing this is you may be very, very "hot" right now and doing a great job. Second place does get a silver medal and in most contests gets a decent amount of money for the effort. So if you want to strive to be the best, you don't need to double your efforts; you just need to up your effort. It may be doing just one extra thing a day. Make one more phone call, read one more page, or give one more compliment. In addition, if you think you do the worst job, know what you know now in this *Tool* you may be "warm." Warm is technically hot, just not as hot as it could be and definitely not boiling.

So use this *Tool* as a reminder of what a little extra effort can do. Understand that the difference between first and second involves a small percentage — and while it requires very hard work to finish the race, it doesn't require you to give an effort that you can't achieve. Use this to understand that if you strive for a good life or the life of your dreams, the extra effort you need to make is just a small, achievable "tick." By setting this mindset up in your brain, you will seize opportunities that arise to turn up the heat just that one extra degree. You now know that for the most part you don't need to double your efforts, only increase your efforts a little more each day.

30. Turn your cell phone off for 24 hours.

This is one of the hardest *Tools* to use in the system and one I am sure many of you will avoid using or see no way you could ever use it at all. With that said, let me ask you a question, what did you do before there were cell phones? I believe we have become addicted to our cell phones to the point that we have become enslaved. Just to give you a perfect example, have you ever seen how someone acts when they lose their cell phone? You would have thought they lost a loved one or been deserted on an island. The truth is if you put half the effort into things like you did in replacing a lost phone, there is no telling what you could accomplish.

The problem is larger than communication. If it was used only as a device to call people and receive calls, we all might be in a little better shape. Today's cell phones do too many things and they often take away from things we could be doing to increase success. Texting, games, music and the list goes on. It is great for me as a chiropractor because people have their heads bent forward focused on their phones; looking on-line, and texting, texting and texting — a plethora of cricks in the neck.

There is a part of success that is known as "present-time consciousness." It means being aware of what is going on around you and focused on the task at hand. Giving your full attention increases the probability of success and growth. There could be someone next to you who you could engage with, who may have a lead for you or a possibility to network. Think of the human interaction you may be missing, or how the statement applies that life is passing you by.

How can this *Tool* help achieve success? Just turn it off and find out. It will be uncomfortable and you will have a lot of excuses as to why you can't. Leave a message that you have turned your phone off for 24 hours and you will call them back. If there is an emergency, in this day and age they will be able to find you and chances are the person right next to you has one. A full day of no phone gives you time to think, look around you, and reflect. You will be less worried about what others are doing, because when you have your phone and think that, you call or text that person. You will feel different, which is a good thing, especially if we try to change habits and establish new pathways.

It is truly an exercise that you can only feel the full benefit by doing it. If it is really too much for you to do it for 24 hours, try leaving it at home one evening when you go out. Or just have a time of the day that it is not on or around you. When I run I don't take the phone. I usually run for about an hour and enjoy personal time where I cannot be reached. Give it a try. You will know it works if you accomplish your goals. If turning the phone off makes things happen in SANE then you know you may be overly attached to your phone.

31. Winners make commitments, losers make promises.

To use this *Tool* effectively we must first establish that there is a difference between promise and commitment. As you hopefully noticed in this book and maybe others, the words we choose can drastically change the directions we head and the levels we reach. Words empower and have some superficial meanings, but words can have deeper meanings on a subconscious level. Thus, we want to distinguish between a promise and a commitment.

We hear the word promise all the time. It suggests we agree to do something and conveys a sense that we tell the truth. The problem with the word is that it can mean one of the two things. Another problem with the word we used it often as children, a time when bending the truth or a fib was commonplace. So over time the seriousness of this word has been diminished. "We promised" as a child when we were not being truthful. Over time this establishes an acceptance that a promise is not something ironclad. We often use the word promise to appease someone. We usually make "promises" in emotional situations and that also compromises the validity of the word. Notice that the word *compromised has promise* inside of it. As I said earlier, this book is written to illustrate what the most successful people do — one is make commitments, not promises. Both children and adults need to graduate from promises and start making commitments.

The word commitment sounds more powerful than promise. People committed to something are all in and usually have an emotional component tied to it. Notice the difference. A promise is made in response to an emotional situation, while a commitment is made because the person has passion about ensuring the desired outcome. Someone committed has more invested than someone who has made a promise. Break a promise and you most likely let someone else down; break a commitment and you let others and mostly ourselves down. Knowing what you know now about making your own reality and that you are responsible for your environment around you, letting yourself down is no longer an option and that is why winners make commitments. So start making commitments and start being a winner.

32. The hole you receive through is only as big as the hole you give through.

There are so many reasons why this *Tool* works and why it is so right. If you are like me, you have witnessed the dog-eat-dog mentality. You have noticed those whose motto is to get as much as they can by any means. On the lowest level, criminals who cheat and steal basically give through no hole and what they receive is very little unless you are talking about jail time. This *Tools* works on multiple levels: The first, and one you may just have to accept on a little faith, is that it's just the way the universe works. It's one of those little-known "secrets" that for the most part rewards those who give just as much as they receive.

On a more practical level, when you give through a bigger hole, you are more likely to receive because others notice. You have a greater chance for referrals, being acknowledged, or just being given more opportunities because people admire your notion of "give first." Keep in mind sincerity is a key; this *Tool* does not work with the sole intention to receive more. I think another reason one receives more by giving more is it enhances one's self image. You will never outgrow your self-esteem. When we give through a large hole, it makes us feel good about ourselves. It is obvious to see that this better self image would only naturally begin to foster success in our personal lives, thus increasing the size of the hole we receive through.

A modern example that I think works perfectly is the mortgage industry. There was a time that it seemed half the people employed were working as brokers. Now most of those people have moved on; there are only a few who survived the crash. Why? Well, the majority of the brokers who jumped on board did so simply for their own benefit; they did it to make money to "get theirs." They put clients in products and loans that they knew were bad ones. The hole they gave through was very small and the hole they received from now no longer exists. On the other hand, I know a few people who survived. How did they do this? Their motivation was to make a profit just like the other guys, but they did so by doing right by the client. So in essence what they have done is kept their existing client base for future business, and they have the ability to pick up new clients by earning the reputation of doing the right thing for their customer. The hole they receive from still exists and will become larger because they gave through a big hole to start. Keep in mind when discussing the hole we receive through, we are not just talking about money. Imagine the good feeling the ethical brokers now have by doing right by their clients. Wealth is measured in many ways.

I struggled in this department as well. I was consumed by insurance adjusters and companies refusing to pay claims. I was constantly worried about things in the office. I often found that all the distractions took me away from the things I enjoyed about private practice. Then that all changed when I put my personal mission statement online and made it my mission to serve others. After that, nothing else mattered much. At the end of the day I would count how many patients I treated and that was how many people I served and lives I changed. When I started doing that, my income and satisfaction greatly increased, hence increasing my wealth, simply by focusing on the "hole" going out, not what was coming back in.

33. What you think of most is what you become.

A large part of this system as you have now discovered is to reprogram the way you think and put in place a system that sets you up with a greater probability of success. This *Tool* is crucial if you need help in this re-programming process. It is widely accepted that the mind cannot tell the difference between a thought and an actual event. Understanding this helps immensely, because it reminds us to continually think of what we want and what we want to become.

There are some simple strategies you can do to help think better thoughts. The first is identifying what you do and don't want to become. It sounds easy but you would be surprised by how many people's goals are just to get through the day instead of building every day. The good news is that you have that accomplished already in your mission statement. So we need to use this *Tool* to remind us to pick aspects in our lives that foster what we want to become. Look at your environment — it plays a constant role in your thoughts. So let's improve that environment to think more about what we want. We need to hang around people who want what we want. We need to read books and watch programs that put us in the mood and direction we strive to go. If you want to be a better person, hang out with better people. It is only natural that you will start to think more like them. If you want to be healthier, hang out at healthy places. Want to be a firefighter, try to hang out with firefighters so you think like they do and know their thought processes.

Those who constantly live in fear most often find new things to be afraid of. If you constantly think every relationship you have ends up in a disaster, then what do you think will be the likely outcome? If you think negative thoughts, you get more negative; think positive thoughts and increase that probability. If you think you are "The Man," you walk around like someone who is and people see it. If you think about winning most of the time, then you will win most of the time. There will be the naysayers. "So if I think like a pro athlete or a model, will I become that?" Well, not exactly, but you may start to think you are better looking or you may start doing some things that most athletes do: train hard, enjoy wins, and help others because of the benefits they have received and accomplished from being an athlete. Whatever movie you play over and over in your head, your brain watches and interprets. If you play a horror movie, no wonder you're only surviving. If you start playing the type of show in your head you want, your brain and life will start to respond accordingly.

34. Walk to conclusions.

There was a point where I debated including this as a *Tool* wondering if it really applied to the system and how it could actually help the SANE section of your blueprint. Giving it more thought, I believe that jumping to conclusions may for some of us be a pitfall that hinders us from reaching our particular goals. When you jump to a conclusion, you can only land in one spot. When you walk to conclusions, it empowers you with the ability to navigate. Implementing this *Tool* gets you out of the mentality that answers are always an A to B equation. You are much more likely to succeed when you realize that issues are not always solved in a straight line, but at times will wiggle waggle back and forth.

Use a slower more systematic approach to reach an endpoint allows us the ability to make corrections along the way. Now that you know how the system works, making corrections along the way plays a large role in the personal growth process. Jumping to a conclusion only allows for one answer, and in life there is not only one answer. The ability to leave options open greatly increases our ability to reach our ultimate destination. The road to success is rocky, but it is the rocks that you use to grab onto as you strive to reach the top.

You may have heard before that when you *assume* things, you make an ASS out of YOU and ME. So when we assume, it leaves us little options for anything else. We need to have options as we go through this process. The bottom line for using this *Tool* is that the question is always an open-ended one. If you always figure things (conclusions) will end up a certain way, then you severely limit the ability for things to grow. Jump-to-conclusion thinking limits us. So on a larger level, we try to change one-track mind thought processes, which is similar to the idea that things don't change or no matter what I do it won't make a difference.

Slow down a bit and walk to a conclusion you have. If you were right, then you will end up where you originally thought you would. But if you were wrong, walking to the conclusion may prove you arrive at a different endpoint. The most important thing is that walking to conclusions leaves you options, jumping only allows for one endpoint. Letting go of the preset destination in absolutes will go a long way in reaching the goals we hope to eventually reach.

35. The road of "someday" leads to the town of "nowhere."

When people near the end of their lives, I have been told that they do not marvel at all the things they have accumulated; they look mostly at what they have accomplished. Knowing this, what things have you been putting off? We are talking about the "P" word (a.k.a., procrastination). Have you caught yourself saying someday I'll do this or someday I'll do that? This is a handy *Tool* to use if you find that you constantly put things off. You can't build a house and make it complete if you say, "Someday I'll get to the plumbing" or "Someday I'll get into fixing X" or, even worse, building the roof. Hopefully the things you have been avoiding are entered in your blueprint's SANE portion. By doing this alone you eliminate "someday" because you work toward that goal in the next 21 days. If you still find that you fall back into your old procrastinator ways, then pull this *Tool* out of the box and let it work its magic. It is a "Power Tool" because it can also be entered as your affirmation, which is probably a good idea if this is a major trouble spot for you.

36. No decision is a decision.

Why do people avoid decisions? Are you a person that does this? Most likely you avoid making decisions because you fear that you might make the wrong one. But making the decision to not decide means you actually made one! If you can choose between two roads and you choose to stay put, don't you see how that allows you to get nowhere? It's almost worse than saying "someday." At least with someday you would be making a choice. Don't be afraid of wrong decisions. A wrong decision can be corrected, a zero decision cannot. As I'm sure you have learned by now from reading this book, it is the wrong decisions we make that help us grow and steer us to the right path in making the correct decision.

Also, guess what? A possibility exists that the choice you make might be the right one. When making decisions, all you do is build. When you don't make a choice on what you want to do with a particular aspect of the house, nothing gets built — and there is no difference with your life. You need to make choices to build.

The way to get the most out of this *Tool* is when you make a decision, you go into it full strength. Almost as bad as not making a decision is making a decision and then half-assing it. When you make a choice, you go all in. At least if it is the right decision, you made the most of it, and if it is the wrong one, you know what needs to be repaired. Lastly, when you make decisions, don't be afraid to go with your gut. Even though we're not totally sure why we have this feeling, we do. I would say in my experiences your gut feeling is right more than it is wrong. Once you lose the fear of making the wrong decision, things will happen. They will happen because making decisions is a large part of building your life and hitting your goals. One thing for sure — no decision is a decision, and no decision equals no growth.

37. Get in the habit of sending thank you notes.

You may be thinking to yourself, how can sending thank you notes help me reach the areas in my SANE section? Well, that all depends on the goals you have in this section. This *Tool* can be a little random; but it helps you reach happiness and success in a number of ways. First, you may be trying to improve your relationships with people around you or adjust how people perceive you. So from the standpoint of self-image, telling people thanks in the form of a card goes a long way in how that person perceives you, no matter how insignificant the thing is that you thank them for. Building a relationship with clients can be crucial for business and networking. When you send someone a thank you card, they will often be shocked; especially it's a response to a simple, small gesture. It conveys to the receiver that you are aware of their effort and you think of more than just yourself.

Your goal may be to give thanks more for the things around you. Giving thanks is a crucial part of personal success because you acknowledge what you already have. We can lose sight of our actual wealth unless we take the time to look around. So we not only want to thank God or the universe or whatever you give thanks to on a larger level, but we also want to thank those around us who help us reach our goals and dreams. A card is a simple way to do this. If you feel that a card is too small a gesture, send a gift basket or flowers. Gift baskets are what I like to do because often you can incorporate a theme that is similar to the realm of what the thank you is for, or you can customize it to something that the individual is fond of.

Lastly, you just may need to start feeling a little better about yourself, or you may want to brighten the days of people in your inner circle. Most people are not worried about material things as much as they relish acknowledgment. If you would like to improve your relationship with your spouse, give, or better yet send, a card thanking him or her for the things they do. You may thank them all the time and that is important, too. But the gesture of taking the time to pick a card, write a small note, and mail it illustrates that you really are thankful. In closing, when you start to do this on a regular basis, you change your mind set by looking for the good that people do instead of focusing on the bad or waiting for them to screw up. Also, when you give thank you cards for actions you appreciate, the person will continue or increase those actions. I say start simple by buying a box of them and making it a point to send one each day for 21 days, and see how it will increase your probability of success on the SANE portion of your blueprint.

38. On the road of change there will be many tempting places to park; clearly define your enemy to growth.

In our blueprint we set goals for the next 21 days that we hope to achieve. We do so in this 21 day format because we now know that it takes 21 days to instill any habit. We also know we can lose any habit as well in 21 days. So along those lines we want to try to identify the pitfalls that we seem to run into that keep us from doing the things we need to be doing. We need to find the things that keep us from building. Knowing where we don't want to go is just as important as knowing where we are headed.

So what are the landmines you encounter when trying to reach your goals? For many it involves wasting time. We play on the Internet too long or watch too much TV. One thing I find when trying to use this *Tool* is you can ask anyone and they know what their weaknesses are right away. And when they tell you what they are, they will get a little smile on their face because these weaknesses have been around for so long. They laugh because they know what these little buggers are.

If you work to improve your nutritional intake, you already know the tempting places you like to park. We all have areas such as late-night eating, sweets and fast food.

If you are trying to improve your exercise habits, what are the stumbling blocks that keep these activities from happening? By identifying these markers, we can try to avoid them and eventually make them non-issues over the next 21 days. By knowing them we can make a choice to do our best to limit our exposure to these roadblocks to success. If you are a snacker, then don't have treats in the house. If you struggle with drinking too much, avoid situations that may bring up that choice. If you find that you are not making it to the gym because once you sit on the couch you're not getting up, bring your workout clothes to the office. The ride can be less bumpy if you just keep an eye out for the potholes. But you can't avoid them unless you know what they look like.

39. Live each day as your last knowing you'll live to 100.

This *Tool* seems to contradict itself a little bit. The natural question would be how do you do this and why do both? I think that is a fair question. Let's analyze the first part of the statement in living each day as our last. When we approach the day in this way, it is another way of saying live life to its fullest. Think about what you would do with your final days or weeks if you knew that to be true. You would live life fuller and not let any moment pass you by. You would be so much more observant of your surroundings and more likely to do things instead of sitting there and letting life pass you by. You would be more in present-time consciousness. You would be much more likely to be fully engaged in what you were doing at that moment, which in reality is how you should be all the time. By approaching each day as your last, you increase the probability of maximizing your life and will be more likely to do the things that bring you happiness and focus more on what you consider success and wealth.

On the other hand, we need to know that the likelihood of living longer than you ever imagined is extremely real. People are living longer, so we must make our way to this milestone by doing daily rituals that ensure we arrive in our later years with multitudes of wins under our belt and the ability to sustain our independence with age. Many believe they don't want to live that long because they don't want to be a burden and that those later years can be filled mostly with pain and problems. Planting that belief in your head almost ensures that you will cultivate that outcome. Start by thinking now about how you will hit that 100-year milestone in a way that will wow the people around you. To arrive at that destination intact, we need to start believing we are going to be there. Knowing that, what habits and attitudes would we change now? A common theme amongst people who live to 90 plus is that if they had known they would live that long, they would have taken better care of themselves.

So we can do both. We can get the most out of life by acting like we only have so much time to leave our legacy while putting strategies in place to ensure we reach old age with the ability to live a wonderful lifestyle. Or I guess you could do the opposite, keep thinking you have time to do it later and then arrive at 100 wishing you had done more when you were younger and that you had taken better care of yourself. Come on, the answer is obvious. So if you think this reminder can help, throw it in your *Tool* section. You will get more out of your time in the present while getting ready for the inevitable time you will ultimately have in the future.

40. If your tool is a hammer, don't make everything a nail.

As I started writing about this *Tool*, I kind of had to chuckle a bit. I didn't realize how similar it was to the title of the Introduction. By now we have all agreed we want to be hammers because we use this as a metaphor to start building our lives. If you also recall, I said hammers can't build alone; they need other *Tools* to help complete the job — and you are learning those *Tools* right now. Understand the lesson that every challenge cannot be handled the same way all the time. If you always use the same approach for every challenge or goal, you leave little wiggle room for the best option to present itself.

For example, working harder is not always the right approach. Sometimes you can adapt and benefit by working smarter. Successful sports teams do this all the time. They come up with different game plans for different teams and different situations. If you're a football team and your game plan is running the ball, you may come up short if you are not willing to throw the ball once in awhile. If you only have one way of approaching things and looking at things, it may hold you back in the growth department.

Another example involves people systematic in their approach to all issues. Everything to them has to fall into an algorithm. If A happens, then go to B; and if A doesn't happen, then proceed to C and so on. Now I am all for systems. I'd better be since this book presents one. A system provides an approach, but sometimes a solution or goal requires you to just go with the flow a little bit. This approach may yield different results for a particular challenge. Describe it any way you want but here is the lesson: When you keep doing it "your way" and "the way it's always been done," you limit yourself, and "your way" may be holding you back. When you deal with situations the same way each time, it limits the outcomes.

41. You have to be there mentally before you are there physically.

Your mind cannot tell the difference between an actual experience and a mental one. This fact is mentioned a number of times throughout this book. I believe this issue comes up repetitively because you need to understand the role your mind plays to determine success. The key to this *Tool* is to start to think about what you want and where you want to be. This is obviously why we write our goals down in our SANE section. We need to use this application to expedite the probability of reaching our destination. Help this occur by thinking about being there before we get there. If your goal is to win a swimming meet, you want to visualize what the water feels like. What it feels like to win the race. How it feels when you hold the trophy. By going through this process over and over in your head, your body starts to feel the event happen before it actually does.

This technique can be applied to other areas besides athletics. If you are trying to build a successful business, what things would you see in your mind that a successful business would have? You would see happy customers buying your product. You would see them sending their friends and family to your business. You would see employees making the extra effort to build the business of your dreams. As you continue to run through this exercise, you start to program your brain to feel what this feels like long before you ever get there. Hence, you start doing the things that make this success begin to feel real and then translate it into reality.

If your goal is to get into shape, what do you think it would feel like to be fit? What do you think you would be doing if you were in the best shape you could be? You would be active and fitting into better clothes. You would be getting compliments from your friends and coworkers. Your confidence would be the highest it had been in some time, maybe ever. When you keep thinking about it mentally, you start to feel what it would be like. When you start by training brain pathways before you get to the actual event, you will plow a way for these goals to actually occur. You can go in many directions with this *Tool*. You might pretend to walk like the most successful lawyer in town would walk. You may fantasize that when you get in your car, you drive that dream car you have always wanted. It works on so many levels. It keeps you focused on what you want, it trains your brain to get used to the feeling of the ultimate destination, and in a weird way you essentially enjoy the prize a little before you actually get there. You get your mind more prepared to accept wins.

42. The four-minute mile.

There was a time when it was believed no man could run a mile in under four minutes. Then in 1954 Roger Bannister became the first man in history to do just that. Shortly thereafter many would come to break a four-minute mile. Now in running, the four-minute mile is considered the benchmark for those who compete in one-mile races. There are other similar stories in human history. It was once believed we could never land on the moon. Before that it was believed that the world was flat and if you went too far, you would fall right over the edge. The proper use of this *Tool* is for you to ask yourself what lies have you bought into during your life? What achievements are you holding back on because someone told you it can't be done?

Over 100 years ago they almost closed the U.S. Patent Office because they said everything that can be invented already has been. I bet we're glad that never happened. Why do people think in this self-limiting kind of way? Remember the described thinking that nails do? People think this way because it is easier, and to reach new levels will require an effort that they have never attempted. People also go with the theory that if they don't have lofty dreams, then they will never be disappointed. I do believe it is important to take an inventory of opinions from people to help you refine and focus your dreams but not when choosing them.

The most successful people of our time became so because they refused to listen to others. To clarify, they went against the accepted norm of the time. Remember the *Tool* we just covered, 41? Well, once the first runner broke the four-minute mile, all the other runners were there mentally. They knew in their minds that it had been achieved and the barrier that was holding them back (themselves/their own minds) had disappeared. They were there mentally, and hence, got there physically. What you need to take from this *Tool* is that the greatest barrier to success is you. You get in your own way. We have programmed ourselves to believe that we can't reach certain levels, and we listen to others tell us things can't be done. Implement this *Tool* so you can start to believe that anything is possible.

43. The baby elephant at the circus.

Way back in the old days, the circus would receive newborn elephants to incorporate into their show. The young elephants had no training and no experience and needed to be conditioned. Even at a very young age elephants are endowed with immense strength and ability to persevere through much adversity. In an effort to constrain this awesome power, trainers would chain these young ones down to keep them under control and teach them early what their boundaries and limitations were. By being chained down at such an early level of formation, the baby elephants were conditioned at a very young age about the boundaries that they could achieve and the limitations their environment provided. Later as adults, these elephants began to accept the limitations that they had been conditioned to accept. Knowing this, the trainers no longer had to hold the adult elephants down by chains and simply used ropes to keep their disciples in line. Those who saw the elephants held at bay by a simple piece of rope were shocked. "Why doesn't that elephant try to run away?" "It could break that rope in a second if it wanted to." You know this and I know this, the problem is that the elephant does not. An animal with the potential to break through the simple restraint that IT has been taught to accept is only real because it perceives these barriers to be real. We see the restraints on this animal as inconceivable because we know it can be broken, but it has no clue of the potential and ability it was born to achieve. There's a little elephant in all of us.

Now we already heard this in Chapter 1. I used this example in the beginning of the book because I think it paints the clearest picture of why we believe what we believe and why the brain thinks like it does. In addition, the reason I repeated it now is because you will be referring to this list to fill out your blueprint. Second, you may just want to share a *Tool* with someone who you think could use one and this allow you to find it in quick reference. For you, the bottom line: Once again we have conditioned ourselves and programmed ourselves to believe what we believe. Break the mental chains that you have constructed over time and watch your wins start to pile up.

44. The definition of "insanity" is doing the same thing over and over and expecting a different outcome.

Want to know what your life will look like five years from now? Don't change a thing. Many reading this book fit right into this statement. You may be wondering why you are where you are — and it's because you keep doing the same thing over and over and you arrive at the same place every time. To break this cycle, you need to try a new approach, and most likely something that is new to you and may be a little out of your comfort zone. If what you have been doing to try and get where you want to go is the same plan over and over, it may explain why you stand in the exact same place as where you started.

Many make the comment they're stuck in a rut. That no matter what they seem to do they keep ending up with the same outcome. For the most part, that is because people are unwilling to try new things and venture out of their comfort zones. Use this *Tool* when you see the rut being a problem with your personal growth. We need to try new approaches when the ones we use don't work. It seems pretty simple, so why don't we do it? The reason is also simple: New things feel strange and awkward. We have been conditioned to avoid things that feel different. So the "bridge" that must be made is that we tread water in our present state and need to find a new way to get to where we want to go. I understand that treading water allows us to survive — and that if we tread water long enough, something may come along. The risk in this line of thinking is that we can only tread so long. Also, when we tread water we stay in the same spot — and that is not where we ultimately want to be. I understand that treading water allows us to survive and that if we tread long enough, something may come along to pull us out. This risky line of thinking means we can only tread so long — and if help doesn't come, we keep right on treading or sink.

Also, when we tread water we stay in the same spot, which may not be where we want to be. As you read this, try and quickly identify if you do this — that is what this *Tool*'s design helps you to do. To shake you a bit and make you see that the reason you are in the same place — the reason you have not been growing — is because you have been doing the same thing over again. Even proven strategies need to be modified now and then to further the advancement process. So if you have been changing nothing, then that explains a lot about how you have arrived at your current place. In addition, if you have been using the same strategy that has worked but now you've reached a plateau, then maybe it is time to shake things up a bit. By understanding that doing the same thing over and over yields the same results, you understand that the process of success requires that you look for new avenues to reach your ultimate goals. No matter your level of success or failure, always be open to better ways.

45. A short pencil is better than a long memory.

The good news about *Tool 45* is that hopefully you've already started doing it. If you have implemented the blueprint system presented in this book, you are writing things down covering multiple aspects of your life. As explained earlier, by writing things down you drastically increase the probability of them happening. We reinforce these new directions by putting them on paper. You can also go back and reference it later. If you feel uncertain about the power of writing things down, have you ever made a to-do list? We all have at least made a grocery list once in our lifetime. Have you ever not bought everything you had on your list? I doubt it. The example seems silly, but on a very remedial level, you greatly improved the chance of buying everything you wanted because you had it written down.

The power of the short pencil extends greatly past lists and goal setting. I remember many times going to speakers and events and just listening. I believed at the time that I would remember all the things that were covered — or if they at least had an outline I would be cool. Studies show you will only remember 10 percent at most, and after a few weeks you will have forgotten 99 percent of the material. So I suggest you take notes at these events, especially if you pay good money for a seminar. You want to make the most out of being there. First, take notes at the event. Then every night after each day of the event, take 30 minutes to rewrite your notes. It will drastically improve your retention and it will assist you in completing the last step.

Send yourself a postcard from where you are at reminding you to type your notes. Most seminars are located at a hotel or have some shop nearby. Just mail it to yourself and write "Type Notes." It will take a couple of days to get to you, giving you time to think a little about what you have learned. Also, since you have rewritten your notes after each day, they will be clear and concise. The final great part about typing them, you will have your own personal resource to be able to go back and visit. Also, if you forgot something, you have the peace of mind knowing exactly where to find it.

You may be thinking to yourself that it will take time. Yes, it will, but you waste time and money when you don't make the best effort to retain what you learned. Enrich your time by spending it well. This theory applies to anything in your life — be it work, pleasure, classes, etc., but if you're doing these things and want to get the most out of them, this is what the successful people are doing. So if you need help in this area, pick this *Tool* and that's what you'll be doing.

46. The best investment you will ever make is in your mind.

I find it very interesting that I listed these *Tools* in no particular order, but sometimes the timing of the order works out as if I had planned it. We were just talking about taking notes at seminars and the like, and how it would improve our lives if we did so. Well, you can't have a short pencil if you have no notes to take. That is why *Tool 46* reminds us that we must invest in our minds to get the most out of life. What exactly do we mean when we say invest in our minds?

Investing in your mind is not expensive. There are lots of ways you can invest in your mind. Seminars are the most obvious. They give you information to improve your headspace and allow you to select from speakers you closely identify with. You may find attending "headspace" events advantageous, because you will be surrounded by growth-oriented people. Remember *Tool 27*? I can't think of a better way to increase business or personal success than by being around like-minded people. To take it up a notch, retreats offer great information, take you away from the day-to-day world, and reduce distractions.

But mind expansion can be as simple as inexpensive books, CDs or videos. Investments in your mind can also help you abstain from the pitfalls that cause your brain to shrink — and we all know what these things are.

When you start to invest in your mind, eventually it starts to pay dividends. As you improve your headspace, the world around you becomes more manageable and things start to happen like never before. The world around you is nothing more than a reflection of what is going on inside of you. When you're a mess inside, more often than not your life on the outside is, too. You will also find mind expansion beneficial to overcome challenges, as they will not seem as overwhelming. If you put a marble inside a tennis ball, it takes up a good amount of space. If you put a marble inside a gymnasium, you would barely know it was there. So start to invest in your mind so you can reap the benefits of that investment.

47. Garbage in, garbage out. Good stuff in, good stuff out.

Gandhi once said, "I will not let someone walk through my mind with dirty feet." Once again we have a *Tool* that plays right off the last one. I swear that I didn't do this on purpose, but I am glad that it happened this way. If we are unhappy with the output of our lives, we need to check what the input is. The way our body reacts is largely due to the things that we put inside of it. I use the analogy over and over that your brain is nothing more than a computer. If you decide to put bad programs, old programs and viruses in that computer, what do you think the screen will look like? If you constantly keep the computer up-to-date with the latest versions and with new and better programs to aid in success and update the virus software, the monitor displays will be much better. Your brain can only work with what you decide to put into it, good stuff or garbage, you make the choice.

This goes for your body as well. You have heard this already, but if your body was a million-dollar sports car, what would you put into it? The best oil, fuel and parts money could buy. You would make sure it never missed a service appointment and keep it as clean as possible. If the sports car analogy doesn't work, let me use a little more serious one. If you had one car to last you 100 years, how would you treat it? This seems to hit people a little harder sometimes; but it's true, you only get one body and the chances of you living to 100 get greater every year. So if we know these things to be true and you struggle in these areas, put this *Tool* to use. *Be the Hammer Not the Nail* intends to help you achieve more wins in your life, hence better outputs. Better outputs start when better inputs occur.

48. Start each day with a GOOD breakfast.

On your mark, get set, GO! This *Tool* works well with *10*, which is *Get up earlier.* We try to get the most out of each day to help us accomplish our goals. We can't do that as well if we stumble out of the starting gate each morning. This *Tool* has so many benefits. The first and most obvious (and aha, once again relates to the last *Tool*) involves filling our bodies with nutrients to get our day started off right. Our body actually decides how to approach the rest of the day based on what we eat to start the day. Start each day with a hearty breakfast and turn on your body's internal furnace, which burns more calories throughout the day. You will also not be as hungry throughout the day and you'll consume fewer calories daily by having this crucial first meal.

If you look at old TV shows, breakfast was family time, it was thinking time. It was a way for people to huddle together and come up with a game plan for how to start the day and then achieve what was on the plan for the day. If you eat solo meet with yourself. Read your blueprint to set your targets for the day. This *Tool* also does not work unless it is a *good* breakfast. I'm not going to get into what you should be having for breakfast. You of course know we're not talking about eating a doughnut or hamburger at a fast food restaurant. You can also have a good-sized breakfast — another cool benefit. If you find you eat too much in one sitting this may work for you. Eating a big morning meal makes you less likely to feel the need to do this at later meals.

I find lunch to be my biggest "high-risk" meal for many reasons. Be it work, being away from home, or just a lack of time, I stumble on this meal the most. By eating a large, healthy breakfast, I sometimes almost forget about lunch, instead of it being on my mind all morning. I also find that I'm not that hungry and can get by with some fruit or something smaller than the full portion I would normally eat. If you want to get the most out of your day, try this *Tool* for 21 days and see the changes that start to almost automatically happen.

49. Do I really need this?

If you have financial challenges and there just doesn't seem to be enough, or you always seem to be falling into debt, this *Tool* will work for you. Something that I noticed was that about a fourth of all things I bought I didn't really need or hardly ever used. I discovered an actual percentage of purchases I never used. So I started asking myself, "Do I really need this?" What I found was that when I asked myself that question, the answer was sometimes no. So I would give myself 24 hours and if I still wanted it, I would go back and get it. If it was too much effort to go back, I realized that I didn't want it that bad or more importantly I didn't *need* it. The pitfall is telling yourself, "I deserve it." We all deserve the things in life, but if you can't weed out the things you need and don't need, you deserve to be poor, too. Happiness comes from the inside, not from things.

The more I learned the concepts applied in this book, the more I realized I didn't have to buy things to make me happy. The impulse pathways that I wired into my hard drive really started to disappear. Asking the question, "do I really need this," does not just apply to material things. It can apply to the over consumption of food. Do I need this second helping of dessert? It can go with alcohol, do I need another drink? It can go for drugs; do I want to put this in my body? The question, do I need this, also asks, why am I doing this? As you apply the principles learned in this book, you will learn and see that you don't really need these things to fulfill yourself. Sometimes curbing our appetites for things we would like to cut down on can be easily done by identifying what we try to fill by indulging ourselves. So if you're trying to cut down on "things" or destructive habits and they have become roadblocks to your success, put this this *Tool* to use.

50. Language is not only spoken; what are you saying?

I have heard this statement before and stated in many ways. I was reminded of it while reading *The Alchemist* by Paulo Coelho. I believe it is an important question because if we try to reach levels of success and happiness, certain things may hold us back that we don't see. We may have blind spots to how people perceive and interpret us. This has some overlap *with Tool 12, You never get a second chance at a first impression*, and *Tool 92, Dress for Success*, but it is unique in its own way. To help you understand what to use this *Tool* for, many areas exist where you express who you are and what you are about — and you may not even know it.

Let's take a look at your house, for example. If we were to walk around your place right now, what would it tell us? Are there dirty dishes lying around? Is there lots of dust everywhere, maybe a few cobwebs? How about your car? Has it not been washed in a long time? Are there empty soda cans all around? Are you still riding on that spare tire? How is your health? Are you overweight, tired all the time, and smell like an ash tray? Do you have decent hygiene? Do you always look like you just woke up? How are your habits? Are you late all the time? Forget to do things you promised to do? Possess the habits of someone who commands little respect?

Obviously we all have cars that need to be washed now and then. There is always some necessary tidying up around the house. You do know the people I am talking about who fit into this category. We often perceive someone who has clutter in their life as cluttered in their mind too. If this person is you, please know it doesn't make you a bad person — and we're not talking about good or bad; we are talking about reaching levels of success and happiness. I suggest if you don't reach your goals and levels of success that you hope to achieve, it may have a little to do with the mess you sit in right now. That mess is *you* — and it is what you "speak" to everyone else. What exactly are you saying?

51. Be on time, don't be late. OBG

Seems obvious but it still seems to happen. This one is also in the realm of *Tool 12, You never get a second chance at a first impression*. But as I said, some stand the test of time for a reason. The bottom line: When you are late and especially a chronically late person, it really says, "I don't give a damn." It says that it was not important enough to be on time. It says, "I had other things that were more important." It says, "I am more important." Bottom line: It is just plain rude.

I am telling you this because that's what it says to me and others. Are people late on occasion for a *valid* reason? Of course. But if this is one of your constant problems, fix it. I've noticed that people who are always late don't mean to be, they just underestimate the time they need. A very simple solution is to figure out how late you usually are, say 10 to 15 minutes. Then just add that to the beginning of when you would get started for work or an event, anything. When you start to be the first one to arrive, people notice. In addition, you can benefit from being on time. A better seat, first dibs at the muffins, but most importantly, you don't rush — and the translation to people suggests dependability and respect for their time.

Remember, we try to use these *Tools* to help us reach our goals. If you constantly show up late to the starting gate, then you will always start the race from behind. Life is hard enough that you don't want to do things to handicap yourself. I think this ties in well *with Tool 29, 211 vs. 212,* meaning you don't have to reinvent the wheel to reach successes and hit new highs in your life. You only need to turn up the effort a little bit — and since most people tend to be late by only 5 to 10 minutes (hopefully), then only minimal extra amount of effort needs to be applied. Remedy the situation by recognizing you are late on occasion, how late and adjust accordingly.

If you really want to get crazy, just be super early every time by a half hour or more, then have something you can be doing when you get there. You could read a book, review your blueprint, go over your wins, and take time to think, or even keep a journal. Notice you have just made time for other areas of self improvement. The bottom line: The minimal effort can only happen if you choose to make it happen.

52. The road to success is always under construction.

Ah, how cute — one of my favorite *Tools*. Did the cover of the book not give that away? This was one of the first lessons I took to heart when I was dealing with my struggles in practice and in life. I was consumed with things that came up and needed to be completed. I was irked by all the things in my office that I wanted to do, long and short term. I was constantly wondering when all these things on my list would diminish. As I finished one thing, another would pop up. When things were going great, then a new challenge to deal with would present itself. It seemed no matter what I did I was never caught up.

There was constantly work that needed to be done, and I felt like no matter what I did it was never enough, and regardless of the effort new things would always be waiting for me around the corner. It weighed heavily on my mind to the point it affected my attitude and outlook on life. Then I was fortunate to stumble across this *Tool*, which in one moment put everything into perspective for me. When you build your life, your work is never done. New areas need to be built — and areas that will need repair from time to time. When you know that this is the case, it gives you a new way of viewing life and prepares you for what's ahead. That's why you have a blueprint in this book to develop plans for what the new areas call for in constructing your life.

You will remember when I was introducing *Tools* earlier in the book that I made the statement that some *Tools* can be considered power tools because of their ability to double up as an affirmation. This is a prime example of that principle. This *Tool* has so much power behind it. You can use it in the *Tool* section or as your affirmation. In fact, this was the first affirmation I used on my first blueprint. You can consider a number of the *Tools* this way. There is no wrong answer. You enter a phrase in the affirmation section that you want to program into your subconscious mind. So I guess truthfully any of the *Tools* could be used in the affirmation section; but in the spirit of what we look for as an affirmation, this is maybe the best example of all the *Tools*; hence the nickname, power tool.

53. For those who believe, no proof is needed and for those who don't, no proof is enough.

If you decide to apply the principles presented to you in this book, I believe this is a *Tool* you will need to incorporate at some time when using this system. This is an adaptation of a quote by Stuart Chase and it needs little explanation. We all know these people, no matter how many studies, how much information, or how many experts say so; they will never believe what you believe. You can waste valuable time and energy trying to convince someone of something that they will never understand. Taking time and energy trying to persuade someone of something they refuse to understand takes time away from reaching the levels we are setting to achieve.

You will run into many who say it doesn't work. They will try to do their best to make you think that your beliefs are silly and a waste of time. Your focus needs to be on building your house, not trying to explain to others how you are building your house. You will only need the proof of how your house comes together. You don't have to prove what you build, but stay true to your efforts. If you need assurance that you're on the right track, the people trying to stall your project will have nothing that they're building. Those who try to ruin your dreams should be thought of as a demolition crew waiting to demolish your creation. How else could you explain it? If you try to reach your dreams and goals, what kind of person would try to stall your blueprint for success? Remind yourself constantly that you are a hammer — and that as a hammer, you build but may miss your mark now and then. Take comfort in knowing that as a hammer you are building, and those who refuse to build their own lives can only feel good about their lack of progress because they can sabotage yours. Your job as a hammer is to build and help others become hammers, but never sidetrack progress on those who refuse to accept help.

54. Track your progress; update your resume or curriculum vitae regularly.

This is a very cool *Tool*. When I used to fill out job applications, I always would forget something I could have included that I had done that might have helped my cause. When you have it handy and check it every few months, the new things you have to add are still in your mind. Some of the things might seem small, but when you add all those experiences up, they make something big. Also, by continually adding new accomplishments and experiences, it illustrates that you are active and working on personal growth. It can be as small as donating your time to charity or attending a seminar. These things show an employer that you have a life and can bring more to the table for their company. As an employer, I can tell you that I find a handful of people qualified for the job. When I see something that says to me that this person is doing more than trying to tell me why they can do the job, I become interested. Have a hard copy you can peruse once in awhile and write updates on it. The key is to keep it handy and update it often, because it is easy to forget things after they have been done.

This leads me to another reason to keep it updated and handy. We have a tendency to forget our greatness because we always focus on our shortcomings. *Tool 24, Review your wins each week*, was covered earlier in the chapter. It is important to review wins because it reaffirms that we do it right, that we are winners. The same concept can be applied by having your CV or resume handy. We want to see our accomplishments because it reminds us of where we have been and the ability we have to achieve.

Now many will say you shouldn't rest on your laurels and you need to stop living in the past. I disagree. I think keeping the feeling of success fresh in your mind begets more winning in the future. I believe looking over our accomplishments reminds us not only of the sacrifices we made to achieve them but how worthy it was in the end. If you don't have either of these or feel uncertain how to put one together, use available resources on how to do them. Services exist to help you put yours together. If you get it done and it looks a little thin no problem. Find where you can apply more effort to beef it up.

Remember *Tool 15, Pick a charity*? Ask around. Perhaps a parent, friend or associate can think of your accomplishments, activities or places you donated your time. Chances are there are few you may have forgotten about.

55. Stop comparing yourself to other people.

If you feel that you lack in the success department, the problem might not be your success but how you measure that success. In my experience, most people make comparisons to others. Here's a little secret that most of you already know: There is always going to be somebody who has more *stuff* than you. If you always try to keep up with the Joneses, sometimes you miss the great things you have accomplished that surround you. When we use others as our benchmark, we set ourselves up for failure.

There is another problem: The other people who you believe are more successful may have their own challenges. So what you might be comparing yourself to might not be as great as it seems. We discussed earlier that happiness comes from inside and not outside. So why would we use external measures to determine our success?

We know we hit new levels of success when we like what we see in the mirror. As we check our blueprint every 21 days, we will compare ourselves to ourselves. When we hit the marks we have entered in our SANE section, we know we win. If we compare our wins to the wins of others, we can always find someone who can top our achievement. The nicest thing about using this *Tool* is when you use it, you find that you are much happier and aware of the things you do have. If you're patient, you will often later discover that the person you wish you were more like actually isn't as appealing anymore. If you stop comparing yourself to other people, you will become so successful in life that the person people will be wishing they were more like is you.

56. Ask yourself, what's the flipside?

I guess another way of saying this is turn a negative into a positive. Many of us have heard this stated in one form or another. This was one of the first few *Tools* I ever used. I got it from my first and maybe favorite "headspace" book. It is called *The Monk who Sold his Ferrari* by Robin Sharma, and it is often the book I will buy for people who are having struggles in their lives. Almost everything that has been a negative in my life has actually led to something better. When my parents got divorced, it seemed like the worst thing that could ever happen. What evolved from that were two new families, new parents, brothers and sisters I would have never had. If you asked me at the time, I would have done anything to keep my parents together. Ask me now, and I could not imagine my life without them apart.

I'll give you another example. There have been times I have prayed to hold on to relationships I have had. Now, I thank God they never worked out. If you practice finding what can be the benefit in the face of adversity, it will keep the bumps in the road as bumps and not pitfalls. I think adversity is life's way of making a correction to get you back on track. Use it as a benefit and it can help you refocus and remind you what you strive to achieve. Dwell on it and just stare at a flat tire that can be fixed. Flat tires are part of life; will you change it and find the next town or be a crazy person who curses at it?

When we constantly try to find the best of any situation, we train our brain for success. We want to enforce positive pathways and chemistry in the body. Find the positive aspect of a bad situation gives us direction for action. By doing so, we are less likely to become stagnant and hence do nothing. It also sets us up for success in the future because we will be better prepared to tackle similar challenges as they arise. If that's not good enough for you, then think of it this way: People would rather be around a positive person who tries to make the most of a situation than someone who sits and complains about it. Also, there is a risk of becoming just plain negative about everything if you're not careful. Be aware, I am not saying make everything happy and exuberant. I'm saying that more than 90 percent of the time you can find some good in any situation, if this is a *Tool* you decide to put to use.

57. When you're ready to quit, remember Yo Pal Hal.

I could give you thousands of stories about people who could have given up and taken the easy way out. The one I have selected is *The Hal Elrod Story* by Hal Elrod. Don't believe in angels? *Believe.* For starters, Hal had some angels looking over him — and second, because I was fortunate enough to meet him. Hal got hit by a drunk driver and left for dead and at one point was dead. Instead of folding like a lawn chair and playing the victim card, this winner came out on top and then used this experience to help others. He fought trough a brutal rehab assignment and when he came out on the other end, vowed to use his second chance in life to show others how to get the most out of theirs.

What's your excuse? Do you have one? Most common excuses I hear point to it always being someone else's fault. I very rarely hear someone who puts the focus on themselves. For the record, I am no saint on this one. There was many a time that I had explanations for why I had a reason to blame someone else or quit. Once again, this is the reason for this book and the *Tools* I am trying to share.

An example I would like to share hits close to home. My nephew Brandon (who rocks by the way and so does Dillan, his brother and my godson) was diagnosed with mild autism. My sister was needless to say devastated. Did she howl at the moon and try to find someone to blame? Nope, Checka (her name is actually Francesca and she spells it Cecca but I spell it the other way and since I invented the name because I couldn't say her name as a kid, I feel I have the first right of refusal) took her opportunity and used her gift as a chef to put together a cookbook of gluten-free recipes to help families in this situation. A gluten-free diet can sometimes help kids in this situation. No excuse, no blame … a prime example of a challenge (not a negative) and turning it into a way to benefit others. And there are tons of these examples: The founder of MADD (Mothers Against Drunk Driving), Coach Jim Valvano who turned his cancer into hope … these people were dealt tough hands and found ways to make them winners, make them missions. Once again, what's your excuse?

We all have general everyday junk. We went over that earlier in the book. You have hopefully tried your best to empty your glass by now. There are many of you reading this that has experienced things that go beyond everyday stuff. Why not use this as an opportunity to do something big? We do our best work when we are motivated or inspired by a tragic event. People want to follow winners — especially when they have stories that seem overwhelming. There is nothing more impressive than someone who comes out on top in the face of adversity. You can improve your present situation and be a beacon of hope for others. This is also known as a win-win. Regardless of your story or excuse, we all have them. So if you find that you kick rocks and feel a little bit sorry for yourself, have your pity party and then ask yourself, "What's my excuse?"

58. Join the "Why Not Club."

Some of you reading this book really need to get out of your comfort zone. It is your self-limiting attitude that creates a ceiling of limitation for winning. I learned this *Tool* from my mentor Charlie Ward. We may be limiting our success because we are not accepting opportunities that come our way. If you want to reach levels you have never achieved, you need to explore some areas you've never been to before. This *Tool* can also help if you need to shake up your routine a little bit. Start to get in the new habit of saying "Why Not."

Saying why not will first be beneficial because you will be creating more opportunities for yourself. These new-found opportunities can be excellent times for growth and discovery. By having new experiences, you open the door to new possibilities. You will begin to see things from new angles. You will regain the feeling that you are living life. From a business point of view, you may just take it as an opportunity to network. You have much greater opportunity for things to happen when you have more outlets for things to happen. If you lack passion for something, you might find a new love or hobby that will help you regain winning feelings. If you have trouble meeting people, saying why not to new things may open new avenues. It's going to feel uncomfortable at first, but remember, growth occurs most in these unknown areas.

This *Tool* can be very helpful if you aim your sights too low. You may have taken advice from others when you set your mark. Joining the why-not club provides strength to set goals that may seem a little crazy or out of reach. Many of you need to start setting your goals at a higher level. You may just hit a few of them. When you start to hit new levels, people will take notice. Many will start to wonder what has gotten into you. As you start expanding your parameters for success, others who never before considered you for a trip or a company position or for a date may now be more intrigued by your new approach at life; hence increasing the possibility for more wins leading to increased success. If you don't feel it right now, just make the words come out of your mouth, "Why not." It will get easier, especially when you start to experience the benefit this *Tool* provides.

59. Live your life like it was on TV.

How would you live your life if it was on TV? That question may be a little easier to answer these days with all the lame reality shows that have evolved. Many of us would act differently if we knew we were being watched. Just think about a time you have been watched, by a boss, parent or security camera. We make better choices when we think we might be being watched. I don't mean that we act like bad people when we know we aren't under surveillance; I simply mean that we make better choices if we think we are being observed.

The benefits are many. It keeps you more ethical. Opportunities to cheat exist all around us. We cheat when we think we won't get caught. Pretend you're on TV and you will be dissuaded from cheating. If you are in an area of high risk for cheating, implement this *Tool* for your benefit. The unethical label is hard to shake.

I also like that this technique keeps you from giving a B effort. We want to give the best we can in all we do every day. It can be easy to fudge a little here and there when we know that no one will notice. The key is that you will notice and we now know how our inside world shapes our outside world. We also want to do what successful people do — and they don't cut corners. Finally, it works with the simple things. If you watch your nutrition and you know you are on TV, you probably won't sneak in that bag of chips while you're all alone.

I realize this may seem silly — and most of us will never be on TV — but this exercise makes us think before we act, which we should do. Think about the action before you perform it. You probably wouldn't do it on TV so then perhaps you shouldn't in real life.

My brother Harry was the one who inspired this *Tool*. He made the comment that he lives his life often thinking about what the people he respects the most would think. What would he want them to see? I really thought this made a lot of sense. It is easier to cut corners when we think others won't notice. To assist you in using this *Tool* do what I do. Over my desk I have a picture of my grandfather and the two godfathers of my profession. By having their images close and "watching," I am more likely to give my best because I wouldn't want them seeing anything else. If you need to change how you "act," live your life like the star of your own TV show, and guess what, you already are.

60. "Don't think, it only hurts the ballclub."

Let's set the scene. In the 1988 classic movie *Bull Durham* the character Crash Davis played by Kevin Costner is acquired by a minor league baseball team (The Durham Bulls) to groom a hot new prospect into becoming a major leaguer. His assignment: Ebby "Nuke" LaLoosh who has a million-dollar arm but a five-cent head. Nuke continues to sabotage himself by always over analyzing everything and in doing so constantly making a disaster of his situation. Realizing this, Crash offers him some words of advice, "Don't think, it only hurts the ballclub."

We all know people who rehash everything over and over to try and make sure they have covered every possibility and outcome. They ask everyone for their advice on the situation and then pose other possible scenarios for response. They run every possibility out to its full outcome, buy books on the subject, and do their research on the Internet. Setting up pros and cons outlines for every decision they need to make, thereby limiting the probability of making the wrong choice. Then what do they end up doing the majority of the time? They have over thought the situation so badly they make the wrong decision or no decision at all. You also know right off the bat if you are a person who falls into this dilemma.

If you find yourself in this manic mentality, my suggestion is to just stop over thinking everything and simply start letting things happen. You also need to understand that if you make a mistake, it is part of the process of success and that the most successful people fail the most as well. When you stop over thinking and just start doing, you achieve that state known as "the zone." Athletes know this mental state all too well, because when you are in it you can do no wrong. You run on automatic pilot. When you ask people how they achieved a particular win in this state, they will tell you they have no idea, they were just "in the zone." So if you are one of these people who over thinks things to the point that no one will even discuss it with you, use this *Tool* and don't think, "cuz you're only hurtin' the ballclub."

61. When the rope gets slippery, tie a knot and hang on.

There are going to be times when we are challenged in life. Things are going to occur in your life that will create self-doubt and shut down the growing process — and every once in awhile things will get so bad it might be very hard to find the will to go on. Winners are judged by how they handle change, challenges and troubled times. Anyone can bask in glory and strut their stuff when things go good. The true test of character comes when the water gets choppy. How will you handle stormy weather? If you can't find an immediate way out of a storm, tie a knot and hold on.

As you go through life there are peaks and valleys. The peaks are a time for celebration and the valleys are a time for learning. I learned this *Tool* from the book *Peaks and Valleys* by Spencer Johnson. This book fell into my lap just as I was writing this book. I coincidently read the book shortly before expanding on this *Tool*. Now Mr. Johnson had been mentioned earlier for another book on handling change. And to be quite honest, I was hesitant to reference the same author again, even if it was for another one of his writings. In this case the message of the book was too hard to ignore, and as the author states himself, "It is a message you must promise to share with others."

The good times and bad times in our lives are connected. Peaks and valleys go hand in hand — where the valley starts to end the peak begins. We need to learn some things about peaks and valleys. If we pay attention to what is going on at these times, we can make peaks last longer and learn how to get out of valleys quicker. In order to understand how tough times are a part of life, we need answers to a couple questions. How do we deal with peaks and valleys? What can be learned to avoid or shorten these periods in our lives? When things spin out of control, grab on to something and hold on the best you can. Know that a peak will arrive — and sometimes just hold on tight to get out darkest of times. You may find that as you hold that rope, a few people might grab your leg and force you to hold on for others too. So holding on for dear life can also affect those in the storm around you. Be strong, hold on, and once that flash flood rolls through the valley, find your gear, clean yourself off, and start that climb to another peak.

62. Happy people work on solutions, unhappy people talk about problems.

By now you know one thing for certain — how you approach life influences what you make of life. Do you choose to be a hammer in life and take control or play the victim and be a nail? How you choose to approach the challenges in your life determines where you go and how long you will be there. Unhappy people talk about their problems as a means to deal with adversity. They often will talk about it to anyone who will listen, even people they don't know very well. Sometimes total strangers become their audience. Why? Friends and family who do know them will avoid them because they don't want to hear about all their problems for the 100th time? Not only do they always talk about their problems, but they always seem to have a new one to talk about. You just want to say to these people, why don't you do something about it? The "problem" with that is it would require finding a solution.

Solutions are more difficult to work on. They require a level of effort that only winners can work on, which is why winners are mostly happy. They don't sit in a pool of problems. They know the amount of time they will be in any particular problem will be short lived. When they have a problem, they instantly start looking for a solution. Even better, when they find a solution to a problem, it becomes a win for them — and that's why they are winners and they are happy.

People who talk about problems use it as a means to get others to commiserate and feel like they do. Instead of finding a way to get out of a situation and the way it feels, they would just rather have others feel the same way. Unfortunately, it's not hard to find others to listen. Remember, there are a lot more nails than there are hammers. You can easily find someone to listen to your problems, because you give them an opportunity to also share their problems with you. To become a hammer you need to build — and to build is a solution. Nails sit around waiting. When you wait and don't act, more problems often come.

63. The problem is not in making mistakes; it is in making the same mistake over and over and over.

Let me cite a remark made by Thomas J. Watson, Sr., founder and former CEO of IBM:

Would you like me to give you a formula for success? It's quite simple, really. Double your rate of failure. You are thinking of failure as the enemy of success. But it isn't at all. You can be discouraged by failure — or you can learn from it. So go ahead and make mistakes. Make all you can. Because, remember that's where you will find success.

— Thomas J. Watson, Sr.

For many of you the risk of making mistakes is so great and so feared that you end up making no choices at all. Making no choices guarantees and ensures very little growth or success. It is hard to build your life when you're afraid to pick up the hammer. Many of you will make mistakes and then make them over and over. We need to learn from our mistakes and apply what we have learned to avoid making the same mistake again.

I believe our fear of making mistakes develops very early in life. If we made a mistake on a test, it could lead to a low grade. If we made a mistake in front of our classmates, it could lead to being laughed at and embarrassed. If we made a mistake with our parents, it could lead to punishment. Now in your parents' defense, some mistakes can cause bodily injury, but for the most part we have been conditioned to steer away from mistakes. You need to reprogram your brain from believing mistakes are a point-of-no-return. In fact, mistakes help you make a correction to help refocus on the ultimate goal. Mistakes help redirect us to point in the direction of our desired destination. Making more mistakes leads us to more success. Some of the greatest minds in this country have been fired or had their businesses go bankrupt before reaching their ultimate level of success. The only mistake in making mistakes is making the same mistake time and time again.

64. Stop being realistic.

How many times have you heard this before? "Come on, be realistic!" Many of you reading this have been realistic for some time now. The reason you're being realistic is for some reason you have programmed your subconscious mind that being realistic is the better approach. Obviously being realistic feels safer — and when you feel safe, you don't have to worry about fear. There lies the root of the issue — by being unrealistic there is an area of unknown. There is an aspect of fear with being unrealistic. Most importantly, when you are unrealistic, a chance exists that you may fail. Failure is a part of life. When we reach *Tool 80*, you'll come to find out the best players in baseball fail seven out of 10 times.

Nails are the type of people who tell you to be realistic because it keeps you as a nail just like them. Hammers tell you to go for it, reach for the stars, and if you fall, then fall hard and dust yourself off for another run at it. We try to make the best we can out of our lives. We try to reach new levels of success that we have never reached before. Very few people reach the top by being realistic. Now I want to keep it real, being unrealistic does not mean being a complete idiot. You do need a small amount of perspective. For some of you this *Tool* really works in two ways. It will help you stop listening to others tell you which of your goals are appropriate and inappropriate, and it will get you out of your comfort zone to dream a little bigger. Many reading this passage have not reached new heights because realism doesn't allow for building or climbing. So stop being realistic and take off the restraints of realism.

65. Rich people believe "I create my life." Poor people believe "life happens to me."

Let me first give credit to *Secrets of the Millionaire Mind* by T. Harv Eker. Also, let's clarify that when we talk about rich, we are not only talking about money. Rich covers all the aspects of life — money, health, family, spirituality, etc. This is a *Tool* that has the potential to hurt some people if not properly understood. To understand what I mean, let's listen to some other statements made in the book. "Rich people admire rich and successful people. Poor people resent rich and successful people." "Rich people associate with positive, successful people. Poor people associate with negative or unsuccessful people." Now this is a well-respected book that has sold millions of copies. Where I believe you can become injured from it is by letting these statements get you angry. Remember very early on in this book we identified that successful people do one thing and unsuccessful people do another. This is another example illustrating that people who act like hammers build their life and those who think as nails believe life happens to them.

Over and over we see examples from different authors suggesting that we ourselves hold the key for what we consider success. This *Tool* provides added insight on how to accomplish the areas that are important to us — and it can be applied in multiple areas. If you believe you create your life, then you will take the necessary steps to build it. If you think life happens to you, then you will wait around to see what happens next. If you think rich people are bad people, chances are you will never be rich. If you find yourself frowning upon people in love, chances are you will struggle in your own relationships. Your system of beliefs has been developed over time. It is this belief system that determines how your brain chooses to perceive certain situations. It is also how your brain approaches certain situations, and thus leads to certain outcomes. If your outcomes are continually the same and you want to change them, change how the brain does its outputs, which starts with changing how the computer works. And that changes by believing that you are in control of your life. Finally, affirm this new belief system by associating with positive, successful people and admire that success.

66. Become more selfish.

I am going to assume for the sake of the story that most of you reading this have flown in a plane at least once in your life. Although most of us don't pay attention, the attendants give a small presentation on what to do in case of an emergency. They tell you if airbags are deployed, put yours on first before you attend to children. I never thought much of it until I was looking for a good way to introduce this next *Tool*. The reason you put your mask on first is simple: If you are not in a good place, you can be of very little help to others. Many of you starting this system have been holding yourself back because you tend to the needs of others. Doing for others is important — and we all have responsibilities. The problem arises when meeting the needs of others interferes with your growth process and hinders your ability to achieve success and happiness.

Societal conditioning suggests we neglect our obligations (hence become selfish) when we work on our own success and happiness. If being a little selfish improves yourself, then in the long run others benefit by you being in a better place. Now the nails of the world love to call people selfish. It is one thing they like to say because it keeps people at their level. Also, nails are afraid to improve themselves and when they see others trying to do so, they know going to the selfish card can really affect someone who is trying to improve themselves and their situation.

The last thing I notice with regard to this *Tool* is that many use others as a crutch or an excuse for not working on themselves. They can't hit the gym because this person needs me or that person needs me. They can't read or take time for themselves because there are too many things that need to be done around the house. They don't do the things they need to do for themselves because the needs of others are more important. They basically use the "martyr approach" for conducting their daily life, and in doing so have a reason why they're stuck in a rut. By approaching the day as a martyr, it gives the person a feeling of being needed and having more self-worth. When they pick martyrdom and those things that "martyr" them go away, they have a problem. As the things they were responsible for disappear (e.g., empty-nest syndrome), they either look for new causes or find themselves lost without others to focus on.

Start to become more selfish and work on yourself. It will feel weird at first but as you start to reach new heights of success, your ability to help others will become greater. So you basically accomplish two goals: self-improvement and better service to those around you.

67. Compile a team of experts.

One thing that has made my life so much easier is constructing a team of professionals to handle the things I need help with to be successful. Identifying weaknesses or areas of needed assistance allows you to focus on more important needs. I am more than happy to use myself as an example. I guess I could try and do my own taxes and save a few bucks, but by using my CPA I know it is done right and enjoy the peace of mind, not to mention the time saved, is worth every penny. Even worse, I am so bad at cleaning my own house that I am embarrassed to say that when I use a sponge, it just doesn't work like it does for others. So in this case I leave it to the experts; I have a housekeeper.

Maybe the best saying is "jack of all trades, master of none." In other words, identify the areas that you would just be better off finding an expert — the value being less stress and the ability to spend time on tasks that help your personal growth. The trick is to find the balance between just being too lazy and spending more time than needed. A personal example, I can do my laundry and watch the ballgame. Staring at the stock ticker and trying to decide which ones to buy, I'll leave that to my expert.

It's a matter of how we can best spend our time and energy. You might be able to change your own oil, but would that time be better spent having someone else do it while you spend some time reading a good headspace book? I don't know what the right answer is, I am asking you. I often find the things people do to save money don't really add up when you compare it to their time. Meaning, if that time could be used for better things that we say we don't have time for, I would think the answer is clear.

Also, if you are anything like me, when I try to do it on my own, I frequently do it wrong. Then I have to bring in an expert to fix it. What I believe makes this *Tool* so effective is the peace-of-mind factor. By having my team of experts, no problem is really ever a problem. I have a person for it and they have worked on it before. Also, it allows me to focus on the thing that is going to most improve my life: myself. So compile your team of experts and as you do, you will find you have more time and energy to work on becoming an expert on yourself.

68. Start remembering people's names.

This is a very odd *Tool*. You may be asking yourself how doing this will help you succeed in the areas filled out on your blueprint. Well, for starters I told you that I would share with you common characteristics and habits that successful people shared, and in my search this is one of them. Another reason I decided to add this one to the list was that so many people claim to be bad at remembering names and wish they could do a better job of it. This is one of those specialty *Tools* we discussed earlier because it can also double up as a goal as well.

Why is it important to remember names and how can this help me reach new levels of success? Well, the reason I believe this *Tool* is important is really not only about remembering names, it's about being present in the moment. How many times have you met someone and a few seconds later you forgot the person's name? Most of us do it all the time. It's not because we're dumb and don't care. We just don't focus on that one moment. We analyze the situation, think about something else, or prepare what we plan to say. By focusing more on that exact moment of name introduction, you will be more likely to remember the name because you will be in present time consciousness and actually hear and listen to the name. So this is not only an instruction on remembering names but being right here, right now.

Now if you need a simple trick I use to help me remember names, think of someone you know with the exact same name. Then upon seeing that person again you will associate them with the person's name you already know. Remembering names opens possibilities. If you avoid someone at an event or party because you can't remember their name, you may miss out on an opportunity. In addition, when you remember a name, it tells the other person that you paid attention the first time you met, which impresses people. When someone remembers my name, I have to admit I am impressed. One, because I am usually pretty bad about remembering names myself and two, the perception I have is that person remembered me for a reason. It doesn't matter why. This person made an effort — and I will remember them. If you convey that to others in business and social settings, it's simple to see how this can add to new levels of success, happiness and the increased probability of hitting your goals. Hi, my name is Lance.

69. Choose the latté or a million dollars.

You feel that no matter what you do or how much you try and save, you're never able to get ahead. I think we all feel like that a little bit. The problem could be not that you don't have money to save, but that there are some holes in the bucket. There are really two principles to saving money. You can either increase the amount coming in or decrease the amount going out. Now increasing the amount coming in can occur but often may take some time, further education and additional training. The easier way is to fill some holes in the bottom of that bucket. When I mention this to people, they always exclaim that they have tightened things up the best they can. I find this may not always be the case. After reading *The Automatic Millionaire* by David Bach, I discovered that you only need to make a few small tweaks to have close to a million dollars at retirement.

We all have things that are comforts each day. Things that we have come accustomed to that we like to think of as our things. They act as our little rewards or treats during the day. Sometimes we just feel we need them. For example, many of us purchase something like a mocha or muffin each day during work. It serves as a start to our morning or a retreat we make with others at break time. Did you know simply cutting that out and investing that money could make you a millionaire? I am not going to go through all the math and compound interest equations to prove it to you. The point is when you feel like there is no way to save you have to really look at your daily habits.

"Well, I deserve to have my mocha each day." Well then, you also deserve to be poor when you get old. Find the holes in your bucket. What needs do you fill with daily $4 or $5 purchases? As always, let's keep things in perspective, I'm not saying that you need to drink tap water and only listen to free radio. I am saying if you buy a couple of magazines a week and a soda each day, you can tighten up and save. So if saving money is hard for you, stop looking at your paycheck and start looking at your habits.

70. Keep an open mind.

Some of you reading this needs to get out of your own way — you probably aren't reaching the level of success and happiness in your lives because you won't let it happen. If you have an open mind, you may get something out of a particular situation or you might not. When you go into it with a closed mind, you are almost guaranteed to get nothing out of a situation every time. Successful people leave themselves open to success while unsuccessful people stay closed minded and reap the same result every time.

Well, if we know that open-minded people have more wins than closed-minded people, why aren't we all open-minded? The answer is simple — open-mindedness leaves you with the greatest chance of reward but also leaves you open to the greatest possibility of failure. It is a prime example of risk versus reward. So being closed-minded limits your chances of looking stupid and making a mistake but you also close the door to success. We don't need to worry about this because by now you should understand that there are no mistakes, only making the same mistake over and over again (*Tool 63*). And if you go into a situation with an open mind, you may just surprise yourself and come out ahead with a big score. So do yourself a favor and go into more situations with an open mind so you can leave more situations with some success under your belt.

71. Sharpen your axe.

There once was an old man who was recognized as the greatest woodcutter who ever lived. In the history of woodcutting, he had never been beat. Then along came a new young buck to the scene. This young man was faster, bigger and stronger and was winning woodcutting competitions all over the land. To prove himself as the best, he had to beat the old man who had never been beat. So the competition began and the young man cut wood with a reckless abandon. As he looked over to see how he was doing against the old man, he noticed many times that the old man often took breaks and during these breaks the old man was cutting no wood. So the young man, making sure he would be heralded as the best of all time, continued to chop away. When the competition was over, the old man had won, cutting more wood than his younger competitor. The young man was confused so when he finally caught his breath, he went to talk with the old man and this is what he said. "I don't understand. I am bigger, faster and stronger than you. On top of that I was working much harder than you during the whole competition, how did you beat me?"

The old man responded, "While you were doing all that work and looked puzzled as I sat at rest, that is the time I took to sharpen my axe."

We have all heard the statement that it's not only about working harder but you must work smarter. To achieve success you need to sometimes take a timeout and improve the aspects that can help improve yourself. This is maybe the best explanation of the system set forth in this book. Having a goal to be the best and enjoying success is great. The *will* to be the best and have success is also great. But you need sharp *Tools* to help your effort and desire to produce the results you shoot for. This means sometimes you need to focus on the basics and take time to work on the things you rely on to make you successful.

If you find no matter how hard you work and how many hours and how much effort you put in doesn't propel you to your expected level, the problem may not be in the effort; the problem may lie in that you have not taken the time to sharpen your axe. In other words, you need to get back to the things that successful people do: reading, affirming, goal setting, working on your headspace, etc. Working on the things that will sharpen your effort will ensure that you reap more rewards from your effort.

72. It takes an hour to burn 500 calories; it takes seconds to eat 500.

"No matter how hard I work out, I just can't seem to lose the weight." The answer may be simple; you might be putting in more than you burn. This is the shortest explanation I have for any of the *Tools*. The amount of time it takes to burn calories doesn't equal the amount of time it takes to consume them. This is honestly good. We wouldn't be around long if the equation was reversed; but over the time of our evolution we have severely limited our need to go out and burn calories, and we have increased the ease with which we can add them. Understanding that our ability to burn is down and the access to consume is cheap and easy, we must apply this knowledge to avoid the temptations that may ruin our efforts.

73. Five percent of the population will disagree with you no matter what.

It has somehow been determined that five percent of people will choose the opposite of anything you say, any stance you take, and anything you believe in. You say white, they say black; or even worse, when you say white, they say, "It's really off white, pearl or beige." Anyway, you get the picture. So when you encounter these people, you have only two choices, sit there for hours trying to convince them of something you never will or spend your time elsewhere. Think about the greatness of this *Tool*. When you stumble upon these people, rejoice that you know how to deal with them — that is, by not dealing with them at all.

Remember you are now in the business of doing the best you can to improve your success and happiness. Know this five percent exists — and when you stumble upon this group of people, limit the amount of energy you spend on them. We want to use our energy to improve our lives and help those people who want to be helped. Spending your time on a group of people who will disagree with you no matter what wastes energy. If you didn't know that this group existed before, you might have made an extra effort in the past. Now you know you bow out early and apply your efforts elsewhere. Do not get hung up on these people. It's our nature to spend extra effort on this group. We believe our extra effort will prevail and win them over to our way of thinking. Not true. We know this because if you were to switch to their way of thinking, then they'd simply change to another paradigm. Just think you cut your bottom line by five percent by eliminating the population that will inevitably choose the opposite of whatever you say, sell or believe.

74. Be a Johnny Today.

Many ask, "How can someone like me make a difference?" Let me share with you *The Simple Truths of Service* inspired by Johnny the Bagger and written by Ken Blanchard and Barbara Glanz. A supermarket chain challenged its employees to do what they could to make a difference in their customers' experiences at their stores. One person left the meeting wondering how he could make a difference since he was handicapped and there was little that he could do, and what would his effort matter for he was only a bagger. So with some help from his family, he decided he would put a positive saying for the day into each bag he packed. Weeks later, many noticed that his line was longer than any other lines to check out from the store. When they suggested that the customers in line go to a checker that was open for quicker service, this is the response they heard: "I want to wait in this line so I can get Johnny's saying of the day."

Many of us fall into the trap of believing we can't make a difference because of our employment, status or physical limitations. The truth is you affect everyone you come into contact with each day. The way you approach anything you do drastically affects the people you encounter. I hope this story illustrates the power you have to affect others no matter what you do or your limitations. If you need a further example, think of those who assist us from day to day. There are many jobs that people can just show up for and get a paycheck. We don't think much about it as long as they do the job to some minimal level of competence. What we always remember are those people who do their job above and beyond the level of duty. My own personal plug, nurses do a job way above the level of what we would consider acceptable. I hope your experience has been like mine that nurses do a job that most of us could never do and they do it at a level that I still have a hard time believing. Making a difference is the hardest when you feel that your job has little influence. Your job is important no matter what your belief about its significance.

This *Tool* applies to any job from the most prestigious to the lowest hourly wage. To be honest, I think it most often applies to the jobs that may feel insignificant. Using a personal experience, I hope to shed light on the power of this application. During the process of completing this book, I had the opportunity to take a vacation to Mexico. On the trip I had the unfortunate luck of breaking my big toe and had to cut my trip short and fly back to the states to determine the damage. Unable to walk, I was carted by wheelchair from flight to flight and from flight to baggage claim. I felt embarrassed — me a big guy with a broken toe. I know, very sad, but I truly couldn't walk. Also for the record, I wasn't drinking when I broke it.

All the people who helped me along the connections were the best. It was the woman at the Sacramento Airport that made me feel like a king. When you have to wait for a wheelchair coming off a flight with a broken toe, you feel kind of silly. When the chair arrived, the lady assigned to take me to my bags was one of the happiest/nicest people I've ever met. She made me feel like I was a VIP and that the injury I had was serious. She cared for me and joked with me the whole way. I just could not believe that she approached her job in such a positive way. She had no reason to do this besides just making the most she could of her job and making my experience the best she could. Her name was Shannon Colman and she made me feel like I was the most important person in that airport. I put her name in my iPhone to make sure I wrote a note to thank her. I hope this does her enough justice. When you think your job is insignificant and you can make a difference, just try your best to be a Johnny.

75. Blood is NOT thicker than water.

The statement should read, "Blood is way thicker than water." Meaning in many cases it can be like molasses and is another area that seems to stunt personal growth. As mentioned in *Tool 3*, just as not letting go of an ex or divorce can be a major obstacle/roadblock to personal growth, a very close second is being held hostage by family members holding the blood comment over your head. Would you have their back for a murder? No. Would you have their back for theft? Probably not. Where is the line drawn? Or do we just keep fixing the poor choices they make over and over again. I think you get the picture. I've noticed that the people who go to the "blood is thicker than water" card are usually family members who need your help to get them out of some mess they got themselves into. The belief that you must be a martyr for family members is a joke. Keep in mind I am not saying family is not important. I am not saying to not help family members. I am saying family members should be a *part* of your life, not your *entire* life.

I often find that people spend little time working on their own lives because they are always busy working on the lives of members of their family. If you will apply this *Tool*, you will start to understand you cannot let family become a roadblock to your success. You are no more obligated to help out a brother or sister than you are a good friend. You may come to find that you are different from some family members. You may find that your aspirations differ from theirs and that your moral standards do not parallel theirs.

Tool 66 states, "Become more selfish." When you decide to shed the belief that blood is thicker than water, you will be called "selfish" by some family members. Remember, people do this to drag you down to their level of unhappiness. If you concentrate on yourself a little more and become more selective as to how you help family members, you will in turn improve yourself. Therefore, by soaring to these new levels of personal highs, your ability to be of assistance to family members in need will be vastly improved. Do not compromise yourself when the line you draw becomes blurred because it has been disguised in the name of family. Family can come first, when the members who need help are also willing to help themselves.

76. Keep a Journal.

Looking back in time, many famous people have found some outlet to write down feelings and experiences. They have been recorded in the forms of diaries, journals or reconstructed from notes into memoirs. We even have modern examples that we now call blogging. What journals do is allow us to write down events that have occurred during the day or week and then our assessment of those events. They allow us to more readily identify wins, understand emotions, and calculate pitfalls encountered along the way. These serve as a great *Tool* to improve success and provide a great resource for us to go back and evaluate feelings and encounters we have had in the past.

Many of you have developed patterns that hold you back. Without identifying these patterns and triggers, you are more likely to repeat them. If we don't learn from our past, we are more likely to repeat it. Keeping a journal helps you see routines that you have established that may be handcuffing you from achieving your goal. Some of you may have trouble expressing how you feel and find it difficult to open up to others. You may feel embarrassed about your lack of success in your life, which is common. You can jumpstart your ability to express those feelings by writing it down on paper. By organizing your thoughts and writing them down, we follow that imaginary connection from arm to brain. Also, you may just surprise yourself at how much you are actually accomplishing. Use your journal to write down daily wins. You may not feel like you have had many wins in your life because you have been conditioned over time to only look at defeat.

If you are at a loss as to where to start, I suggest you purchase *The Winners Journal* by John and Pam Carls. I began journaling with this tool and continue to use it to this day. It has many helpful exercises in it to help you stay motivated and on track. The first mission statement I developed was with the help of this book. Also, their affirmation of the day is posted clearly in my office for all to see. If you want to start the process of using a journal and are not really sure how to start, you can't go wrong with what the Carls have put together. They also provide (as this book does) other suggestions of what to read if you are thirsty for more knowledge on this subject. Almost all the successful people in the world in history and present day find ways to write down their thoughts and feelings, what they have learned, and where they hope to go. Take advantage of this *Tool* of expression that helps you learn more about you.

77. Laughter is one of the keys to life.

There is an old Japanese proverb that states, "Fortune comes to those who smile." Laughter has been shown to possess many beneficial qualities to the human body. Laughter can lower your heart rate and reduce blood pressure. It has been shown to free up respiratory passages and harbors the ability to reduce pain by causing a release of endorphins that are 10 times more powerful than morphine. Laughter reduces stress, increases immunity, contributes to better sleep, can help with constipation, and can even lead to a better sex life! A good laugh will burn 3.5 calories. Laughing increases oxygen intake which invigorates cells. There is one problem though. First, people smile only 35 percent as much as they think they do. Also, a child laughs or smiles 400 times a day, but by the time an adult reaches 35, that number drops to 15 times a day. The bottom line, people, is that we need to start laughing a little more.

Happiness is a choice. So we can be happier by laughing more and we can laugh more by the decisions we make. When you decide to go to the movies, just pick more comedies. When you do watch a limited amount of TV, choose a comedy. You could probably cut your TV time in half by selecting only funny programs. If you have satellite radio, turn off the news and only listen to the comedy channel. A simple way is to go on www.youtube.com and search for your favorite comedian. If you don't have a favorite, let me suggest Jim Gaffigan and his standup on bacon. He is one of the funniest guys on the planet. When things in our office need a boost, we throw this on to give us all a laugh. Statistics show that people are 30 times more likely to laugh in the presence of others than just by themselves. So make your way to a comedy club. We all need to laugh a little more, but laughing more sometimes requires a little work.

78. Learn a new definition each day.

By now you have hopefully begun to understand the power of words. The words we choose to put in our head and the ones we use to describe ourselves build the foundation for how we traverse the challenges in life. If we hope to increase the power of the words we choose to describe ourselves and increase our probability to reach new levels, we must increase the number of words that we understand. To expand the ability of our own personal computer known as our brain, we must provide it with the ability to do so. This comes from increasing our vocabulary to give ourselves more power for success.

There are many ways to achieve this *Tool*. The simplest is to look up a new word in the dictionary each day. The key to doing this is just like this book's system; do it daily and consistently. Maybe you do it in the morning as you sit down to breakfast. If you have a family, you can do it at dinner so everyone learns the new definition. You may even let a different family member pick the word that night. I know there are also desk calendars that have a new definition each day. How you do it doesn't matter as much as doing it and doing it in a consistent format.

Successful people choose their words carefully; but to have words to choose means you need to increase your ability to do so. This daily ritual can go a long way in many areas in which you try to achieve success. In your work and school environments the benefit is obvious. Expanding your vocabulary increases your ability to communicate — a crucial component to success in work and scholastics. It also enhances your ability to increase awareness in the world around you. When you clearly understand what you read or hear increases your ability to take more information away from interactions. We also want to know how best to describe ourselves now and who we want to be. Our mission statement provides that foundation. The better words we can choose to fortify that statement provides the ability to build a stronger foundation, thus allowing us to build bigger and better projects for our life.

79. Be a student and a teacher.

I love that people in the "self-help" industry tend not to be selfish. I truly believe they are motivated by helping others be the best that they can be. How do I know this? In many of the books, CDs and videos I have encountered, one of the statements constantly made is to be sure to share your new found knowledge so you can help others. They almost always insist you share the information that they just gave you with others. Most of us find great joy in assisting people to improve their lives. This book was born by taking what I have learned and then incorporating it into my own system that I believe makes the knowledge user friendly; but before I became a teacher, I was a student.

It took some time to acquire the knowledge I am sharing with you. The process of a student is an important one. I forgot after grad school that your days as a student never end. You need to understand this idea as you try to reach new levels of success. You need to understand that you will always be a student — and if you acknowledge that fact, you then must find places to go and learn. Being a student means going to class. When I say "class" I mean metaphorically speaking. For you going to class is any opportunity you can find to better yourself. This can be in reading, writing, listening, etc. These opportunities have been around all this time, but you didn't know where to look and probably didn't think you were still in school. Many of us were poor students so the idea of continued learning may be scary. If this is so, the thought of being a teacher may be even scarier.

If you want to become smarter at any trade or acquired knowledge, teach it to others. In grad school when I finally made the decision to be smart, I took the opportunity to tutor others on the knowledge I had already mastered, and in doing so it became even more concrete in my head. In the same respect, by sharing the headspace knowledge I have learned with you, I in turn have begun to own it more. It is becoming lodged into my subconscious mind. So you must also be a teacher. By sharing your knowledge, you help others and help yourself.

80. An all-star in baseball fails seven out of 10 times.

If you have a .300 batting average in baseball, you are most likely an all-star and if you end your career with this kind of average, you are likely headed to the hall of fame. To have a .300 batting average in baseball you must get three hits for every 10 at bats. This means seven out of 10 times you will have failed. Failure is the highway to success and failure is learning how to win. When you start to understand that the process of failing has a direct correlation to winning, failure doesn't hit you as hard as it may have before.

There are a ton of examples of people who failed in the world and it was their perseverance that helped them succeed in the end. A famous story that many of us have heard about is the one involving Walt Disney. Disney was rejected for his ideas over and over again. If he hadn't kept swinging his bat, we wouldn't have the happiest place on earth. When a baseball player gets a hit, he tries to identify what he did with that swing that helped him succeed. When a hitter strikes out, he heads back to the bench and has some time to reflect on where he went wrong. What is for sure is that he will live to swing the bat for another day. You must continue to show up at the ballpark and take your hacks for the fences. There are times you will hit a homerun, there will be times you strike out. There may even be a time you get hit by the pitch; but one thing is for certain, you will never get a hit if you don't step up to the plate.

81. You don't want it bad enough!

For most of you, this should be the first *Tool* you ever choose. This *Tool* is maybe the best example of how the system works in the whole book. Many of you have had a goal that was never written down or reached. Many have written down their goal and still failed to reach it. I believe goals have a greater chance of success when you have the proper *Tools* to help you reach them, and this one is a perfect start and example. I love this one — it has great power to keep you on track. Whenever you are about to do something that may sidetrack one of your goals in your SANE system, simply say to yourself, "I don't want it bad enough." When you make this simple statement, it triggers a reaction in your brain to determine if you do want it bad enough.

This can be applied to many of your goals. If your goal is to read one book a week and you are watching TV instead, ask yourself, "Do I want it bad enough?" When your alarm goes off at 5:00 a.m. and you're about to hit snooze, ask yourself how bad you want it. When you cut out dessert and you feel tempted to have that bowl of ice cream, do you want it bad enough? Sometimes getting the right answers out of life requires asking the right questions.

You may find something else out: *You really don't want it bad enough.* Then comes decision time. Do you take it off your goal list or tweak it to match what you do want? If you find out it is truly not that important to you right now, then take it off. This may be the reason you miss some of your goals because they really aren't goals you hope to achieve at this moment. If you do decide it is something you want, you will have constructed a mindset that allows you to make better choices when presented with temptations. Asking yourself how bad you want it determines your likelihood to achieve that goal. The things you want badly enough compel you to do what is necessary to reach the top.

82. "I worried about a lot of things, half of which never happened."
— Mark Twain

It was strictly by coincidence that this *Tool* follows the one listed above. This may be the second one you want to put on your first blueprint because for many fear may be the number one thing that holds people back from growth and success. Mark Twain said it right, many of the things we spend time worrying about never happen. So why would we waste our time and energy on them? The best thing to do would be to focus our energy on what we know and then deal with things as they present themselves. Fear can hamstring us in many ways. Let's look at why we want to stop worrying and stop fearing.

Fear holds us back from making a decision. And as you remember from *Tool 36, No decision is a decision.* We've learned we need to be in the business of decision making — we grow from our right or wrong decisions. We no longer fear bad decisions — they are the pathway to success. Eleanor Roosevelt said, "You gain strength, courage and confidence in every experience in which you really stop to look fear in the face. You must do the thing which you think you cannot do." How right is that statement? If you fear you can't do something or worry about all the bad possible outcomes, most likely you will avoid that opportunity. We should run to fear and use fear to motivate us. Use fear to our advantage. We strengthen outcomes if we also stop worrying so much about all the things that can go wrong. Things will go wrong now and then if you worry about them or not. Here is the million-dollar question, though: What if everything goes just right?

Since this *Tool* is a quote, I thought it appropriate to sprinkle some others in. H. Jackson Brown said, "Don't be afraid to go out on a limb. That's where all the fruit is." That limb may break and if it does, you'll dust yourself off and try again; but if it doesn't, then wow! What a sweet reward for yourself. Some of you may need to just start climbing up the tree and that's OK. Marilyn Ferguson said, "Ultimately we know deeply that the other side of every fear is freedom." I hope this *Tool* will set you free to let go of your fears and stop worrying so much because ultimately it can be one of the greatest roadblocks to success. I'd rather be a lion for a day than a sheep for life.

83. Stop stomping on sandcastles.

We remember playing at the park in the sandbox. After taking some time and a little effort we constructed a beautiful sandcastle that we were excited for all to see. Most of our classmates congratulated us on our achievements and encouraged us to keep building; but there was always that one kid who shortly after sharing your new creation found the need to go Godzilla on your sand sculpture and stomp all over it causing it to come crashing down. I always remember thinking as that kid walked away with a smile, why would someone do that to someone else? Nothing hinders personal growth as much as hindering other people's growth.

Sometimes when we aren't in a good place in our lives, the only way we think we can make ourselves feel better is to bring others down to our level. If we have trouble reaching success, we find it necessary to criticize the success of others. It is a defense mechanism we use to explain why we avoid trying to build our lives. For example, if you were to get a new car that you were proud of and your friend found the need to tell you all the problems and costs associated with that car, it is their way of avoiding striving for success. They associate success with additional problems and responsibilities. It is just easier to find a way to bring others down than try to reach success of their own.

By starting the process of being happy for others and their achievements, you associate success with good feelings and relinquish bad thoughts you have trained yourself to feel. You will shortly discover *Tool 88* that will express the benefits of teaming up with others to reach new levels. By congratulating others and showing true excitement for their achievements, they are much more likely to include you in future endeavors. They may also share with you some of the secrets they have learned that have helped them along the way. One thing is for sure, if you are in the habit of stomping on people's sandcastles, at some point they just won't show you them anymore.

84. Listen to motivational CDs.

This is maybe the easiest *Tool* to use in the box. There are no instructions needed. Let me start by asking you a question, how much garbage do you listen to each day? News, gossip, reality TV, etc.? And you wonder why you are a negative person? Or do you at least wonder why you aren't reaching new levels of success? This is one of the most obvious. Media ironically tells you bad news and provides information on depression so you too can become depressed. Then they give you lots of commercials to tell you how to fix your media-induced depression and sickness with a pill. If you truly want to reprogram the way your brain has been wired, then think of this *Tool* as antivirus software.

Many spend a good portion of their days commuting to work. We all connect commuting with something bad, something negative, or something we hate and wish we could avoid. Why not use that time for personal growth? What I hear a lot is, "I don't have time to listen to CDs or read these helpful books." Hello, it's not that you don't have the time; it's what you do with your time. If you commute an hour a day ... well, you do the math. Another great time to listen to these motivational gems is during your workouts. If you are the type who likes to multitask, then here is a perfect opportunity. Think of the opportunities you have that you could replace with listening to positive CDs or the possibilities to do two things at once. Does anyone here garden or have lawn work?

When it comes to people who don't utilize motivational CDs, I believe they either never have listened to them or maybe dabbled a bit and quit because they didn't work. Well, if you've never listened to them, then you have no excuse not to try this time-tested *Tool*. For those of you who have and think that it didn't do much for you, I may have a theory as to why. A *Tool* can only build if you have the plan of what to build. This is why I have you fill out a blueprint so you have a plan and a direction. I think many believe they can just pop in a tape and everything should be better and when it's not, they say the audio "self-help" stuff doesn't work. If this is the case, give it another try as it applies to the SANE system. When you listen to motivational programs and think about what you have written on your sheet, this *tool* becomes more effective — you directly apply their advice to the goals listed on your blueprint. When I have goals written down and fresh in my mind for the next 21 days, the CDs have a much more profound effect. Selecting the speakers that are right for you is like picking a hammer that fits just right. Chances are you'll find a few.

85. Ultimately, you choose.

Sorry if that hurts, but it's true. You have the choice, what you eat, who you date, how much you drink, who your friends are, what you listen to, how you react, what you accept as truth, *you choose*. When there are situations that arise that seem (and may be) out of your control, you choose how to react. I also understand and agree that we may encounter challenges that are more difficult — challenges we may not have brought on ourselves. Depression, for example, can be due to some faulty wiring. Alcoholism and drug addiction can also be a disease, but ultimately you choose whether or not to use the means available to you. You have to grab the life vest if someone throws it to you. We can blame no one but ourselves for the outcomes of our choices. Just understand that ultimately you choose — and if you make choices that take you to the wrong place, find a way to change it. When you really grasp that *you choose,* you stop blaming others and make better choices *or* find the *Tools* or resources to help you make better choices.

This *Tool* really is a two-step process. You accept that life is all about choice and that ultimately you choose. Part of this first step involves understanding that happiness is also a choice. You need to choose if you want to be happy or unhappy. When you finally make that choice to be happy, then you move on to step two and begin by making the choices that bring you happiness. This means making the choices that will ultimately make the goals listed in your SANE section become reality. Just writing them down is not enough; we need to make the choices that will make them occur. If your goal is to get up at 5:00 a.m., then you may have to say no to some things at night. If your goal is to cut out sweets, then you must choose not to have them in the house. If your goal is to watch less TV, then you must choose to not turn on your TV or maybe even more drastic, choose to turn your cable off. Awareness that we are nothing more than the choices we make, makes us more aware when making a choice. You are always one choice away from changing your life.

86. You can put some people up in a castle and they will complain the floors are made out of stone.

Some people will complain about anything. For the most part, whatever you do to try and accommodate them, it just never seems to be enough. They have two cousins we have already discussed, *Tool 73, Five percent of the population will disagree with you no matter what, and Tool 83, Stop stomping on sandcastles*. We all know right now a person in our mind that fits each one of these three descriptions. You probably know someone who encompasses two or maybe even all three. There is also a small chance that these attitudes may have described you. What makes them all important *Tools* is that all three types of people and all three types of thinking are almost guaranteed to impede success. If you have gotten into the habit of doing these three things, then the easy step is to stop. If you encounter these types of people, do your best to avoid them. We want to become hammers and builders. These types of people will keep us distracted from the task at hand.

These three scenarios all encompass what one would describe as no-win situations and from this point on, you are not going to put yourself in a situation that cannot produce a win. Our last *Tool* basically reaffirms that you choose. You can choose to weed these people out of your life because that is what you do with weeds — pull them out. Also, know that you know that you can choose to be happy if you want to; you feel a little better by avoiding these types of people because that is where they *choose* to be right now. No matter what you do, they have to make the choice to want to change their approach and way of thinking. I find it very liberating that you can improve your own life by turning off the noise makers that try to distract you. Use this *Tool* in two fashions: to help you avoid being this type of person or as a reminder to avoid this type of person. Either way, negative mindsets will slow you down. You can drive with your parking brake on, but wouldn't it just be easier to drive with it off?

87. Stop acting your age.

What I notice most about people who try to act their age: They seem to become a little boring and take fewer risks. When you act your age you also act how you *think* people your age should act. People who tell you to act your age are probably similar to those who tell you to be "realistic;" remember *Tool 64*? When you act your age, you limit your ability to grow, have fun and enjoy life. There is a balance, though. Keep in mind we are not talking about being irresponsible. We want to encourage a no-holds barred attitude you had when you were younger that allowed you to discover new things. The ability to try and go for it because you weren't as worried about what others would think. The balance occurs when you can apply the knowledge you have accumulated as an adult while never losing the twinkle in your eye that you had when you were young.

What are the benefits to using this *Tool*? Thinking young expands your options. When you don't try to approach everything like someone your age would, you open yourself to many more opportunities. Why? Because the simple statement of "acting your age" suggests that you should try to act more mature, think things out, and make decisions based on safety and realistic attitudes. When you try to act your age, you make decisions according to what people your age would do — and we are not trying to do what people our age would do; we are trying to do what successful people do.

When you stop acting your age, you will find that you will be open to newer and more experiences because you don't base your decision on what your peers would decide. Those who tell you to act your age do so because they believe it can limit the possibilities of making mistakes. We now know that making mistakes is crucial to growth. I think lastly and most importantly, acting younger just makes you more fun to be around. If you want to reach levels and goals you never have, being fun to be around can only help. When people want to be around you and fall in love with your spirit, it feels good. When you feel good, you like who you see in the mirror and affirmations become easier and more believable. The take-home message: Acting your age boxes you in and takes decisions out of your hands and puts them into a checklist of what is OK and not OK for the others similar to our time bracket.

88. Form a Master Mind Group.

There are support groups for all types of things, including groups for alcohol and drug abuse, overeating, grief, parenting, writing, etc. Having the support of others and knowing there are others going through the exact same things as you will help the process. Support and therapy groups offer different perspectives to help members overcome obstacles. We can use this same principle to help us build success. We can also help foster success in others. I am talking about forming a Master Mind Group — and it is a *Tool* I learned when I read the book *Think and Grow Rich* by Napoleon Hill.

A Master Mind Group is when a handful of people in a similar field or with likeminded goals meet to share ideas on what works and what doesn't. The group "Master Minds" on things they can do to be more successful, and in doing so they put working principles in action while avoiding ones that don't work. In addition, people can share advice with others on challenges in their particular business.

There is plenty of wealth to go around for all of us. Do not be afraid that you will be divulging a secret to others. Remember *Tool 32, The hole you receive through is only as big as the one you give through*. I have learned so much while "Master Minding" with other professionals in my industry. I don't really believe that there is any competition. If you worry about what you are doing, then it doesn't matter what anyone else is doing. What I mean by this is construct a group of people who do what you do and are the type of people who you respect in your particular field, industry or belief system. By helping each other you all win. And if you are in a competitive field that you can't share with the guy next door, form a group with people from other states. Once again, remind yourself that you are trying to accomplish more wins and successes. By getting together with like-minded people who are also trying to reach new heights, you will all climb higher by tying up and climbing together.

89. Keep in touch.

"It's been too long" or "We need to do this more often." One of the lamest things is losing touch with friends and family. The key to not losing touch is to make it automatic. Have a family reunion that is the same time every year. Have a dinner night with your dad that is automatic every week. Have lunch set with friends on Tuesdays every week. One trick I like to do is to scroll through my phone list on my cell phone in the car (no accidents please, follow all local and state laws) and call friends and family members. Or have a time that you make a call to one old friend each week. The reason for this is obvious: If you don't make it automatic, you end up saying things like, "Where did the time go?" Also, these people can help and support you in achieving your goals. If you have negative friends who don't support you, I suggest you lose them, but if you can't, just don't call them as much. This goes for family members too (*see Tool 75*).

Keeping in touch can also assist you in having a successful life. We want to live our lives with no regrets and with the feeling that we have built something and left a legacy. People commonly regret toward the end of their lives having not spent enough time with family and friends. Achieve this goal by keeping in touch. This *Tool* assists you to keep avenues open so that more opportunities can arise.

In addition, friends and family may notice a change in your new approach and attitude in life. This will also help with reaching goals because others will be more likely to help you along the way. Warning, there may be some, on the other hand, who try to stall your growth or are jealous of your newfound vigor. Be aware you may need to distance yourself from these people because you now limit contact with people who sabotage your path. Lastly, and most importantly, it just feels good to keep in touch and when you have more things in life that keep a smile on your face, it can only help the overall scheme of things. Now put the book down and go call someone you've been meaning to talk to.

90. Get a theme song.

Just like you define your personal mission statement, you need to develop your national anthem. Find a song that you can play to get yourself psyched up. In addition, you can find songs to meet different needs, relaxation, thought, love, time out, etc. Bottom line: Find songs that kick start what you need. For example, I used to listen to metal and punk to get ready for football. I would put on dance music when I was going out. I love to listen to 1970s music to get a smile on my face. When I was running my first marathon, I played "Rocky" on repeat for over an hour to get me through the final leg. When I was in fourth grade, I remember my mom listening to Barry Manilow's "Ready to Take a Chance Again" and explaining to me about my future stepfather (who by the way is one of the greatest men I have ever met and who I consider a father).

Songs can also be great ways to bring you back to feelings in your past. I can remember being in the back of my dad's Vette listening to Billy Joel. When I walked up to my first high school dance, I can remember hearing "Money for Nothing" by Dire Straights. I also remember hearing "You Had a Bad Day" minutes after a girl had broken up with me. Bringing up old feelings can help bring back feelings you want to avoid and launch emotions that can be used for growth. That is how this *Tool* works its magic; it sparks feelings.

The strength of music is its ability to move you, and the movement that most of you need is motivation. Many of you need to find a way to propel yourselves into reaching your goals, and finding the right tunes can be your catalyst to do just that. Find the music that motivates you. Find a song that can help define who you are and where you want to go. I mentioned earlier about using music to complete my first marathon. I compiled a list of songs that got me pumped up.

When things got really tough at the end, I simply repeated one song over and over to help me finish the race.

This strategy can be applied to many other areas. You may not know it, but many of you have done this before. I believe most of us have listened to music to help us get through a long drive. Music is used to inspire religion, celebrate a wedding, and even to remember those who have passed.

I think to best use this *Tool* with regard to success is twofold. First, make playlists to help you course through areas listed in your SANE section. They can help you get through a workout, start your day on the right foot, or even help you in your times of relaxation. Second, just as you pick an affirmation to be your mantra for the tone you hope to set for your blueprint, picking one song to be your theme song or personal national anthem can also set the tone for keeping your mindset where you want it to be. I described earlier how we correlate music with times in our lives and feelings we have had in the past. We can use this connection with music and mind to place us in the headspace that will best set us up for success. Find the song or songs that would best describe the country known as *you*.

91. I am not alone.

I thought long and hard about how to most accurately describe this *Tool*. One of the key components of this book is understanding and accepting that the illustration that is your life is for the most part determined by you. Your present situation has been constructed by the habits and attitudes you have harbored up to this point. When you begin to accept that your present situation is largely due to circumstances that you alone have created, there is the pitfall in believing that you are alone. Ultimately, understanding that we control that path we choose to take leads us to the thought process that we are traveling this path solely by ourselves. Hence, the belief that we are alone and there is no one who understands what we are dealing with. This statement is partially right; we do carve our destiny by ourselves but we definitely aren't alone.

The feeling of being alone is one of the biggest roadblocks to reaching success and personal growth. When we have the feeling that no one understands what we are going through, we feel as if our situation is different from everyone else's. When we buy into this thinking, it gives us the biggest reason for making excuses. Subscribing to the belief that no one understands what I am going through leaves the avenue open for copouts and blame. The truth is you are not alone. The path you are going through, no matter how rocky, has been travelled by many before you and many more to come. So using the *Tool "I am not alone"* gives us the strength to persevere.

Few people take the exact path up or around the mountain, because there are only a handful of paths that can be taken. Some will take the easy way up, some will take the long way, and many of us will encounter traps, dead ends and runarounds, but someone has been down your path. People with similar experience will want to help you. This can be someone from Alcoholics Anonymous, someone in a similar job, a stranger, or whatever you consider God or a higher power.

This is one of those truths that I think is cool about life: Someone who has been where you are before and will share techniques to navigate out. While they can't do the work for you they can help. Once again, you are not alone.

Caution, people are willing to throw you a lifejacket, but they can't make you grab it. The first step in using this *Tool* is to understand you are not alone. The second step is finding the group that has been around your area of the mountain. Then understand that the only way you will end up alone is to continually avoid help that exists and help others try to provide. You will find plenty of room on top of the mountain. People who make it to the top can help but only with those people who help themselves.

92. Dress for success. OBG

Clothing does not make the man or woman, but it sure does help a lot. Think about the times you knew you looked good and how it changed your confidence. You acted a little different, you moved through the room a little different and people noticed it. Some would say when you look good you feel good — and you are in the zone. This can go for the work environment or a social one. This all comes back to the same things that we have been discussing throughout this entire book.

Developing strategies to help us reach goals and reprogramming that space between your ears to work for you and not against you.

Keep in mind I am not talking about *Tool 12* on making first impressions, which is more geared toward forming impressions upon other people and has more to do with just your clothing decisions. With *Tool 92* we are talking about the perception you have about yourself. Admit it, when you look in the mirror and like your outfit you say to yourself (or maybe out loud), "I'm looking good." Does this ring a bell? Doesn't this sound like a positive affirmation? If you had any doubts about how affirmations work, this may strengthen those beliefs a little. This can go for all types of clothes from jeans to a tux. So if you are in sweats and a T-shirt most of the time, you will probably feel like what sweats and a T-shirt provide; comfort but not a lot of confidence. There is a catch to this Tool. If you are out of shape, it is difficult to make certain outfits look good. No problem, right? We have that covered in our SANE system. The best way to start using this *Tool* is to try to find outfits you have that you like and that make you feel confident, and to get out of the clothes that are simply used to "get through the day." We are no longer just getting through days; we are building success each day. So you have to show up to the construction site in your work boots, not your underwear.

There is another way to give this *Tool* some bite. You are going to love this one. Go to the mall and buy some new outfits or even better go for a completely new look. The best way to spark a sluggish mind is to change its routine *(Tool 102)*. So by trying a new image you accomplish that. What can also make this fun and rewarding is by tying it to a benchmark. When you hit a target weight, go and reward yourself by purchasing some new clothes. If you suffer from having too many clothes and risk getting yelled at or in debt, I tell people when they buy new clothes or accessories — something comes out of the closet to make room. Even better, donate it. If you know you are going to have to lose some outfits to get new ones, it makes you think twice if you really want to buy it. One thing I like to do is buy a new shirt for the weekend to go out in. Not very expensive and it makes me feel good about the night to come. So try this out if you need a boost of confidence or just to shake things up a bit. When we look good, we feel it and act on it; and when we're in a better place, the world around us reflects that.

93. Make a superhero.

Ever since we were kids we have been fascinated with superheroes. As children, we marveled at the abilities they possessed. Their superpowers enabled them to be in situations that seemed impossible and under the direst of circumstances. We were so enamored with these mystical powers we did our best to pretend what it would be like to have them ourselves. Their influence on us was so profound it could even persuade us to eat spinach. As we became older, we lost our fascination with their superhuman characteristics and started to become more "realistic" that these abilities were farfetched and few and in-between. This *Tool* will try to convince you that these strengths can become real, if you want them to.

To truly understand the power of superheroes, we must understand the message they convey. Things such as truth, justice, strength and ability to rise to any challenge. Superheroes teach us to tackle desperate situation even when the odds stack against us. They teach us the right thing is always better than doing wrong. And maybe most importantly, you can always learn a lesson from every situation. Modern superheroes live among us — and their powers have been chosen and developed over time with determination, focus and effort.

So the moral of the story: You too can be a superhero. You can choose the superpowers you would like to possess. Now I must be honest, I can't in good conscience tell you that you can fly around the world. I do believe a person can achieve anything he or she sets his or her mind to do. For now, let's just try to determine some abilities that we would like to develop.

What would you look like if you were a superhero? It might be the ability to never procrastinate. It might be the strength to avoid confrontation in a single bound. You may decide to have superhuman ears to listen more than you speak. Or maybe you decide to become Hammer Man and share this book with all who could use its assistance. (Just thought I would try and plant that seed.) Draw up the type of person you want to be and identify what that person would look like — and that is the definition of a modern-day superhero. One that determines how they can be the best they can be while helping others.

Do remember all superheroes have their kryptonite — just as we all have our own pitfalls and distractions. Never fear, because knowing what your kryptonite is helps you become stronger. It lets you know what areas to avoid and which people may possess these power-draining devices. By defining your superhero (see your mission statement) you are more likely to save the day in the end.

94. Find your alternative.

If you are trying to get to the next level of health, we need to stop using drugs and surgery as the first line of defense and the only answer. *Let me be super clear here. I am not medical bashing and I am not against modern medicine or medical doctors or medication when needed. I have had many surgeries. I work with many doctors.* I believe the majority of doctors would agree that their patients need to start taking responsibility for their own health. When I get a cut on my finger, it heals itself. When I get a bad cut, I go to get stitches.

When at all possible we should look for health from inside out, not outside in, whether it be meditation, yoga, massage, chiropractic, acupuncture, physical therapy, etc. It makes me feel good to know more people look at health in this way, which includes nutrition and exercise. Unfortunately, we now eat food products — that by all accounts — are not considered food. Many studies illustrate those under alternative medicine care have lower healthcare costs and get sick less.

Look at how we rank in the world with regard to health. In a recent study by the World Health Organization, the United Stated ranked 37th![3] In my practice, I make it my 100 percent goal to get my patients in optimal health. If I cannot provide that in my scope of practice, I will find (and have done so numerous times) the right practitioner to assist that patient. All doctors, regardless of specialty, are under immense pressure. We must work together to promote health. If you need a population sample for proof, look at professional and Olympic athletes. They use all resources to help them reach optimal performance. Why can't we all come together to do the same for the rest of us?

[3] "U.S. Health Care Rated 37th Worldwide, CBS News, http://www.cbsnews.com/stories/2000/06/20/world/main207853.shtml.

How can this *Tool* assist us in reaching our goals? The answer is simple: When we feel our best we are more likely to do the necessary steps to achieve them. This is why I use Olympic athletes as a concrete example of those who apply alternative medicine to help them reach peak performance. What I believe makes us apprehensive to try these methods is the definition that describes them, "Alternative Medicine." The thought of using the "alternative" can suggest using something that is secondary. And by our nature we want to try a primary approach before moving to a secondary one.

Second, calling it "medicine" instills the belief that in some manner it can solve all our problems. Methods of health that are considered "alternative" are not the sole answer to any problem, and neither are medicines or drugs. As a chiropractor, I believe everyone can benefit from an adjustment to remove the nerve interference in their nervous system. I also emphasize to my patients that chiropractic cannot solve all their problems. They must incorporate multiple forms of care, nutrition, exercise and headspace to reap the maximum benefit from all of these components of life.

While all of these aspects are beneficial to optimal health, they can only express their true benefits when used together. Chiropractic will not solve all your problems. Nutrition will not solve all your problems. Self-help books will not solve all your problems. And "modern medicine" will not solve all your problems. There is a saying, "Everything in moderation." I would change it to: "Everything in combination." Meaning, when all these aspects are applied to work in harmony and when necessary, we will all be healthier and will have the strength to tackle our challenges.

95. Stop reading the newspaper and tabloids.

I am going to apologize in advance to the feelings this may hurt or to any of those in the print media. (Understanding the success of this book may depend upon periodical reviews, I may be biting the hand that would inevitably feed me, but I am obligated to tell you the truth.) In my experience the people who need the most help are those who make a daily ritual of reading the newspaper or subscribing to tabloids. There, I said it; now let me do my best to explain why.

The first complaint I hear from many is the lack of time they have to do the things they know they need to do. These would include reading books, exercising, taking time for themselves, and working on their own lives. Those who engage in reading the daily paper take time from other aspects of their lives that could be used to reach goals and improve overall happiness. Many claim they are also hindered by money. Regardless of how cheap they can make a subscription to a local or national paper, this cost could be applied to other areas of necessity.

There is also the issue of bias. Most modern publications are no longer objective, thereby leading to their inevitable failure. Understanding that there are two sides to every issue, if only one side is mostly represented, the other side will simply stop reading and stop buying. Many people have said to me, "How will I know what is going on?" I would say in my experience, if there is something I need to know, most people will be talking about it.

Reminding myself of issues that everyone already knows exist does little to help the problem and improve my personal growth. Also, if we are trying to become "green" and reduce waste, does this form of information make any sense? Doesn't it contradict this new paradigm shift? Most importantly, garbage in, garbage out; meaning, you ultimately choose what you decide to put in your head. Unless you are a stock broker, why would you ever read the business section? Leave that to an expert who does that for a living and give yourself the headspace to work on more important things, namely yourself.

There are only two ways I know of to make you feel better. You can work on yourself and do the best you can to improve your situation, or you can concentrate on the downfalls of others to keep yourself above them. This is the only thing I can think of that fuels the existence of tabloid media. Focusing on the flaws of others distracts us from our own shortcomings and provides an excuse in meeting our own hopes and dreams. Can you imagine the difference we could make by having positive books or messages at the checkout counter?

Instead we are bombarded with who looks better in a particular dress or who has put on the most weight. What if we had fruit instead of candy at checkout? Life is not only about identifying where you want to go and what you want to be. It is also about avoiding pitfalls along the way. Every time you go to the store, they have two huge landmines right in your way. It's no wonder we are so distracted. This *Tool* is not about having your head in the sand, but understanding that what you may be reading has your entire *mind* in quicksand. You now understand that you choose where you decide to step.

96. Make gossip positive.

We all do it. I do it. We do it so much we don't even realize we're doing it. Gossip deeply intertwines in our daily fabric and becomes almost impossible to avoid. We do control how we choose to engage in this almost inevitable ritual of daily life. Identify why we gossip. It is much easier to talk about the lives of others than to work on our own. Gossip makes our shortcomings more tolerable, but in doing so does little to improve our own situation. We can change this by making gossip a positive interaction. Meaning, if we can flip gossip from being a session of focusing on the negative aspects of others to defending or offering other perspectives to a situation, we can enhance the possibility or probability of making a gossip session a positive session.

You will enjoy many advantages by approaching gossip in this way. By making an effort to make gossip a positive event, you influence the perception that others have of you. If people perceive you as finding the best of a bad situation, it will definitely increase your personal success. This *Tool* will also help you. By mentally making the effort to not find the worst in others' situations, you increase your ability to work on finding solutions to your present challenges. You probably now understand the overlap in many of these *Tools* — and you cannot avoid how they intertwine. You will shortly discover *Tool 100, Focus on yourself*. In making an effort to avoid gossip or making it as positive as possible, you enable yourself to accomplish both.

Finally, we do our best to become hammers and build our own project. We can't build what our blueprint calls for when we constantly focus on someone's flaws. If you would like to increase the value of the home you are trying to build, it would only stand to reason to help your neighbor build their house as well. Those in history who are defined as leaders and winners earned that title by helping those not able to help themselves.

WARNING: This *Tool* is hard-to-use and can cause injury while learning how to master. This *Tool* is also one of the hardest to master in the book and the attempt to use it shows a great effort on your part. While I believe we can almost never master the art of this piece of equipment, I know it can never work until you decide to pick it up. Sometimes you will use it quite well and other times you will forget that you even have it in the bag. Using it may cause you to lose some friends and family who don't believe it even works. Proceed with caution understanding many have never even seen it. To even choose to use a *Tool* of this magnitude will require both a little courage and some sanding against the grain. The secret to make this *Tool* easier to use is to believe that courage can be defined by helping those that can't (or aren't present) to defend themselves. Making gossip positive carries the same weight as standing up to a bully.

97. You will always remember what came hard and mostly forget what came easy.

As I arrive at this point of the book, I have begun to realize that there is a risk I am taking. As I try to provide *Tools* that I believe are necessary to help you reach your goals, I may ruffle some feathers along the way. The dilemma of sounding like Mr. Perfect and a know-it-all can really turn people off. Let me reassure you, I am working on myself as much as you are trying to do. I find it necessary to explain because if you fall short of your goals you might feel like they seem too hard to reach. I believe this is a great starter *Tool* because if you use this to begin any project, it helps you understand its hard work to build the life of your dreams. As you look at the life you have built you will remember the most the areas that took the most effort. Appreciation of this crucial principle of building will motivate you to gravitate to the toughest of challenges and avoid the easiest of paths. It's easy to keep this *Tool* short and sweet. I bet you can name three things right now that you had to scratch, claw and work hard to accomplish. It will take you time to remember the things that required little effort. When you also set goals too low, you just might hit them.

98. Never settle for anything less than you are capable of achieving.

I'm glad this *Tool* comes later in the list because for many of you it can provide insight to why you are in your present situation. A gap exists for all of us, which is bounded by what we settle for and what we can achieve. You are in control of 99 percent of the equation, and knowing this gives you a lot of room to play with. Also, in an effort to be honest, truthful and realistic, we may have certain limitations on what we can achieve. So let's all agree that we can't all be a pro quarterback or the first woman to land on Mars. I am not saying it can't happen but for the sake of argument when it comes to people like you and me, we are attempting to discover what we can achieve and how to avoid settling for anything less.

When we leave this Earth, some of us will pass instantaneously. The other group of us will have some time to look back and reflect on what we have done with our lives. A common theme I hear repeated over and over is the wish that a person had done more with his or her life. The common regret expressed is that they wish they hadn't settled. Time and time again they feel a void because of their inability to reach their full potential. At this time of self-reflection, realizing they didn't become the best that they could be, instead settling for what they thought was OK. Why do people settle? Well, when we settle we tread water. When we tread water we're almost guaranteed survival; however, when we tread water we only do enough to keep our head above water.

So why incorporate this *Tool* into your blueprint? Because the biggest regrets in life are those who settled for less than they could have become. There is no reward for settling because you are accepting a level that you have already achieved. When you strive to reach what you are capable of achieving, you have a chance of accomplishing what you deserve. You may hit the mark just a tad below the top but above the settling point. Or you may have settled and never realized what you could have achieved if you hadn't. I have rarely met someone who went for it and completely missed it. I have heard many stories about those who regret they never tried.

99. To eat an elephant, you cut it into little pieces.

This *Tool* has been described before in many different fashions. Another version you might recognize is, "The Journey of a 1,000 miles begins with one single step." The affirmation I use to help me remember this crucial lesson of life is, "Tomorrow's results start today." The important point: The goals we hope to achieve take many little steps and pieces to achieve them. And when all those steps and pieces are put together, they add up to that distance or become enough pieces to build the likes of a giant.

With regard to the system in this book, remember we are building a home that represents our life. This home takes time to build and for many of you it has never gotten off the ground because you were never given plans on how to build it. The process goes step by step. We decide what kind of custom home we want to build and where we want to build it. Then we work on our foundation, also known as our mission statement. Understand the time it takes (21 days). Then re-inspect your areas and move to the next. Also keep in mind long-term goals for the house in the Roman numeral section. We also have our goals we build right now in the SANE section, and finally we pick *Tools* that provide the greatest likelihood that the project can be built without a hitch.

This *Tool* can be a little misleading. Remember, our journey never ends. We will never arrive at our destination and then have all our work behind us. No matter how many pieces you cut the elephant into, there will always be a section to work on. This is no different than our home, and no different from our life. Remind yourself to take steps to build your life, and your life always requires work. You will also learn two important lessons: First, work on our life is a daily process. When we work on it daily and don't take days off, it will most likely resemble what we want it to look like. Second, the building process is always ongoing, so while it feels like you are always working to try and stay ahead, you do just that. As mentioned earlier, no secrets, drugs or shortcuts — life requires daily work; the key is working smart combined with working hard.

100. Focus on yourself.

If you wonder why the dream life you try to build isn't really coming out as you had hoped, maybe it's because you're spending more time watching others build and not enough time working on your project. Why do we do this when we have a home to build on our own? Up until now you may not have known how to build your own life house. And now you do. This will also help explain why others are so concerned with what you are doing. They either have no clue what they are doing themselves or if they think you do, so they may be trying to copy some of your newly acquired skills. Hopefully, once you begin to become a master carpenter with regard to the skills you have learned in this book, you will hand them a copy to let them know this is where you learned how to build. In doing so, you have helped someone build their own life and "focus on themselves." On the flip side, if they don't use it, you can continue on guilt free knowing you can throw a life preserver but you can't make people grab it.

We can also lose focus as we take comfort in the knowledge others have the same issues as we do. We make ourselves feel better by knowing others have the same problems. Remember we call this group *nails*. We must remember we want to build and become a hammer — and a hammer focuses on itself. A hammer's only concern involves building and not what the nail does down the street.

Every moment you spend working on someone else's project is one less moment you could be working on your own. We often will take breaks or timeouts during the tougher parts to build in our lives. To be a hammer means knowing that working on it right away helps it from becoming a much bigger problem. Being a nail means finding someone else with the same problem and sharing it with each other. This commiseration ensures no building or repair occurs. Nail, nail, nail! You become bigger nail, bigger nail, bigger nail. Bigger nail, bigger nail, bigger nail! Or you may decide to find someone with bigger issues to make yours not look so bad, or blame it on those who have no issues stating that they are lucky. You become bigger nail, bigger nail, bigger nail. Bottom line, when you focus on someone else, you take time from working on yourself; seems pretty obvious to me.

101. The will to win is nothing compared to the will to prepare to win.

Luck is when preparation meets opportunity. Or do you believe some people are lucky while others are unlucky? Even though statistics can't prove everything, people will reference them to explain how luck exists. Most "lucky" people set themselves up to be lucky. Translated, most people who get good fortune set themselves up to win. Two principles are "lucky" people don't always advertise the *Tools* they use to get lucky. Second, people who aren't "lucky" don't do what lucky people do. They also affirm what they are not doing by cursing the "lucky" guy or gal.

Just by the fact that you acknowledge people are lucky or not adds strength to the premise that the universe favors some over others. So with that said, what is more likely? Some people are just *randomly* lucky, or the people who put in the necessary work are more likely to be lucky? While random luck happens once or twice, someone who is lucky does something that allows that to happen more frequently. At least concede you have a better chance of getting in the show if you try to buy a ticket, which means you have a better chance for luck with some preparation.

Successful people for the most part work smarter and harder than those who don't. Harder in my opinion means working on it every day. Smarter only means you have a system in place that will increase the likelihood of success. So you prepare to win by doing it daily and systematically. All the components in your blueprint comprise those aspects made in this statement.

I will give you a classic example. It is common knowledge that Jerry Rice is the greatest football receiver of all time. You might argue that he may have been the best player in the history of football. Experts acknowledged his talent as the best over his closest rivals. It is well-accepted his will to win would have been enough to make him the best. You may be interested to know that Jerry Rice also trained off the field harder than maybe anyone in the history of football. His will to prepare was almost greater than his will to win.

Time and time again I see people who think they can just turn it on when needed, which is not what the most successful people do. If you want a successful life, defined by what success means to you, establish daily rituals, habits and attitudes. You have to want it bad enough and be willing to put in the work when people watch or not. This is the mark of a true champion. Jerry Rice did 99 percent of his best work when no one was even in the stands.

102. The best cure for a sluggish mind is to disturb its routine.

Your brain is like a computer, and a computer can only work based on input and wiring. We earlier covered how the things we believe, shows we watch, and things we read serve as input for our computer. When these inputs equal garbage, it is little surprise that the output matches the input. Our daily routines establish how we approach each day. Routine builds the wiring pathways over time in our brain. Routine repeated each day becomes "hard wired" in our brain and affects the brain's ability to do things other than what it has been conditioned to do. The good news is just as these inputs can be changed, we can also rewire the pathways that exist.

Some simple things you can do are to change some everyday things around you. Rearrange the furniture in your house. Change when you go to bed and when you get up in the morning. Mix up a bit what you have for lunch or find a new place to go. Change the way that you drive to work. When I drive to work I have two options. I can take the quicker route that has a major three-lane merge to make in a small window. It can get annoying because many times others won't let you over or speed up on you when you do. I found myself getting a little angry at these people. So by taking the earlier exit, which takes me about five minutes longer to get to work and has a few more lights, I arrive to work in a much better mindset. Also I used to get to work just minutes before we started, and so I was rushing and trying to make every light and had a sense of urgency to not be late. I now get up much earlier than I used to, thus allowing me to take the longer way to work, starting my day off right, and changing the outcome at the end of my day. Changing routines may show you an easier way of doing things or they may just make you feel better about your day.

We discussed earlier that change is uncomfortable and that's why we choose to avoid it. We also mentioned that if you want to know what your life will look like five years from now, don't change a thing. By shaking things up and moving this around, it gives you new perspectives and allows you to see things in a new way. This is why a change of scenery for people often jumpstarts success. It allows the brain to break the wired chains it has developed over time and gives you the opportunity to work on goals and achieve them. Unless you know to change your old routines, you never will. So implement this *Tool* if you try to get out of your current rut.

103. Supplementation is a must.

This seems like an odd *Tool* to be used to help you achieve your goals and increase the probability of success. Well, if you remember earlier, we discussed that it is most likely these days you aren't fueling your body properly because the components the body needs no longer exist in many of the foods we eat. In addition, it is this lack of vitamins and minerals that cause our bodies to have a myriad of problems that didn't exist in the greater numbers they are today. We want to reach goals and to do this we need to set ourselves up for success. We need to give ourselves every opportunity possible to put the plan we have blueprinted into motion. Otherwise if we are sick, sluggish or tired, we will be less likely to take ourselves to the next level.

Supplementation is a big area for debate. Many people believe that there is no benefit to taking vitamins, herbs and supplements. There are others who claim they can prove that they work, with studies and placebo groups. I believe the truth may have a few folds into it. Vitamins can only work if they are "bio-available" for the body to absorb. From the people I consult in this department, there are vitamins that exist that do provide benefit. Also, while certain medications don't work for all people, there may be herbs and supplements that can benefit us all as well.

I think supplements are a small price to pay for benefits with very little risk. With any preventative measures we take for health, we may never truly know their benefit because we have no way of knowing what problem we didn't develop because of the healthy habits we chose. If we take antioxidants, will we truly know the cancers we avoided? Once again, supplements are a piece of the puzzle. If your goal is to improve your overall health, you will probably be more likely to avoid missing workouts if you pay money for supplements. If taking vitamins correlated into you becoming more active, I'd say that alone signifies a benefit of their use. You must do the homework, but take the time to find what supplements can benefit you and your goal for a better life.

104. Get a Coach.

This was a life changing *Tool* in my life. When I graduated valedictorian of my class and with a perfect 4.0 grade point average, it seemed just natural that all the other pieces would fall into place. The truth was that I was failing and considering the unfathomable possibility that I may have to close my practice. I am so glad that I swallowed my pride and realized while I may have known everything about being a doctor, I knew very little about running a practice. I found a coach who helped me run my practice more efficiently, but more importantly helped me run my life more efficiently. If you take a look at the credits I give this book, I credit a man for saving my life. It is because of him I learned all that I am sharing with you and that I have restructured into a form that I believe can help so many more. Everyone in my opinion needs a coach.

Joe Montana had a coach; Michael Jordan had a coach. These are the top two people in the history of their field and they both had coaches to help them achieve the highest levels they aspired to reach. There are two benefits to coaching. The first is coaches can identify troubled areas you are unable to see yourself. The second is coaches hold you to a higher level of accountability than you hold yourself. If coaching wasn't important, then why wouldn't teams just let the players run themselves? Yeah, I laughed out loud, too.

Finding a coach is not something you just look for in the phonebook. There are a couple of things that I believe are crucial to finding the right coach. The first is a question to ask yourself, "Where do I need help?" I mentioned in *Tool 67* to compile a team of experts. These are people who help you with day-to-day activities. They can be considered all the support people of a team's operations; but a coach sets the tone and develops the strategies. For many of you a life coach may be exactly what you need — someone who can start by overlooking everything. For others you may just need a coach to handle challenges in business, nutrition or exercise. Maybe you need a knitting coach, whatever the case may be find the area that you need to rise above and reach the top. It may also be the area of greatest struggle.

I think it is nice to have a coach with similarities to your situation. When you best identify with someone, you are much more likely to follow their advice and give the extra effort needed to make that coach proud. As you will learn, you do it for you, not the coach. All you have to do is follow those at the top, those who are the most successful have coaches who help them get there. Golden Joe had one, Jordan had one, and I have one. Identify where you need the most help, exercise-trainer, nutrition-nutritionist, self-life coach. Once again, as I said in *Tool 67,* find experts to help you reach your goals. Identifying where you need help is a major part of the growth process. The next *Tool* will help put that into perspective.

105. Celebrate your flaws.

"You know what your problem is ...?" Flaws are not a problem, not knowing your flaws is. There are two aspects to flaws. The first one suggests you don't know your flaws. As we build our life, there will always be areas that need repair. Sometimes we don't know what needs to be fixed. Now as I just mentioned, a coach can help us find our flawed areas and then help apply goals and strategies to repair these areas, which is exactly how the life-building process works. But you can't fix what you don't know needs fixing. Oftentimes we could ask those around us what they believe are the areas we could use a little work on. Be sure when doing this to ask someone you respect who will give you an honest answer. Also, don't pick someone who doesn't have the guts to tell you what you need to hear.

We also celebrate our flaws by understanding that some flaws aren't flaws at all — they are characteristics that make us who we are as people. Many of these flaws without modern miracles or drastic plastic or personality surgery cannot be fixed. You may have a funny laugh, weird ears or just find something about yourself you don't like that no one else even notices. The risk comes when we become fixated on these so-called flaws. In doing so our flaws take crucial mind time away from other areas we can really do something about. The most successful people in the world find a way to laugh at themselves. When you do this you relax about some of the things you may not like about yourself. There are flaws that we need to work on and then there are flaws we need to embrace. When you use this *Tool* to do both, you improve areas that need change and stop wasting time on areas that don't need to be fixed.

106. To get what you've never had, you must do what you've never done.

For many of you the thought of taking steps to improve your life seems overwhelming. Where do you start? What do you do? What happens if it doesn't work? All these thoughts of self-doubt will inevitably lead to one thing: You doing nothing. There is also another possibility. You may do the things that you have done before which haven't worked and lead you right back to where you started. We use common approaches because they feel comfortable and familiar — and we like comfortable and familiar things. When you do familiar thing you end up right where you are now. To get the things that you have never had in your life, you need to do things that you never have done before to get there.

If you struggle to reach the levels of success you desire for your life, how could you see it any other way? *Be the Hammer Not the Nail* is the first step. Using the system in this book is a prime example of doing something you have never done. You must be constantly doing new things to reach the levels you hope to achieve. This is why we change our blueprints every 21 days. We do this to DO what we've never DONE. Human nature resists new things because they feel weird or uncomfortable. With practice this becomes less and less uncomfortable — and this is a large part of what our blueprints force us to do. It doesn't stop with this book either. The process is ongoing and you will have to seek out other new areas to pursue and focus your efforts. A strong focus gets us what we've never had — new levels of success.

When we do what we've never done, it covers many areas. First, doing what you've never done means taking your effort up a level to where you have never been before. Many believe they can't do much more than they are already doing. We will change this affirmation today. We can always turn it up a degree. Working harder is not enough. We have to have that work focused and headed in a common direction, which is how we bring in our blueprint. You will not only be working at a level you never have but you'll also be more focused than you have ever been. Combining an increased effort with a honed-in effort greatly increases chances for success. Understanding that having what you've never had means doing things you've never done creates an understanding in your mind that doing what you're doing now is why you are where you are right now.

107. Get a lucky charm.

I must admit in a book like this it would seem strange that we would be talking about lucky charms. As I stated before, we make our own luck by doing things that put us into a position of being lucky. My lucky charm is an old tie clip from my grandfather that has his initials JBM. I take it with me from time to time when I feel I need a little extra strength for particular situations. As you work through your blueprints, you are going to need help. This help comes in the form of your blueprint and *Tools* and while we have made an effort to make these readily available, we may need a little extra reminder when we don't have our sheets with us — and lucky charms help us with this problem.

I choose one that can be worn or carried around in my pocket. I suggest you put your lucky charm somewhere it can be readily available or out in the open where you can see it a number of times a day. A lucky charm helps you do three things. It symbolizes your desired change and reminds you to focus in that direction. This symbolism is a key to the growth process. As we begin to retrain our brains, the reminder that we build our life helps reprogram new and positive pathways in our mind.

Second, it serves as a constant reminder. When doing any new system, especially in the beginning, it can be easy to lose track of the new effort we make. Having a lucky charm to remind us that we aren't snacking anymore or that we want to be a better listener gives us the greater possibility of achieving the goals on our blueprint without having it taped to our forehead. We need to be reminded that we have goals *and* of the effort we are putting forth.

Finally, the lucky charm serves as a silent affirmation. Every time we see it and touch it, it lets us know we are doing the things we need to do. You can also keep it simple and use your lucky charm as a reminder to state your affirmation every time you touch it. Regardless, a lucky charm can possess special powers if you know the right way to use it — and now you do.

108. I want to be more like_____.

They say that imitation is one of the highest forms of flattery. I guess the key is to choose wisely when we imitate. Wanting to be more like someone else can be a great *Tool* granted that the choice meets certain parameters. The choice can best be made when we choose someone not for who they are but who they've become. When I look at my mission statement, it resembles a person I hope to become. I have found that my mission statement closely relates to what my grandfather was like. I never designed it to be that way but looking at it, it closely resembles the way he conducted his life. He is definitely in the top five individuals I would have chosen when applying this *Tool*.

There are a few factors that should be considered when choosing who you would hope to be more like. The first is not to pick someone who is famous for their power, money or looks. These people most often have reached the top solely on power, money and looks. While there are many famous people who do many wonderful things, I think a more powerful choice would be to choose someone less famous and one who hits closer to home. I think the person who you want to be more like should possess the habits and attitudes that you hope to instill in yourself. What habits do they possess that have led them to their success? What attitudes do they foster that have led them down the path that they have chosen? When you choose to be like someone who has mastered these two abilities, you have a silent mentor to model and shadow. Copycats will succeed when they copy someone with the habits and attitudes they desire and when they emulate the mission statement they strive to achieve.

109. Insert your *Tool* here.

A *Tool* can only be useful if it helps build what the plans call for. I hinted a while back that I don't have all the answers. There are no experts when explaining how one can be successful in life. What teachers use in this genre is proven strategies to help you become your best and then add their own personal twist. Then I believe you will gravitate best to the person who explains the message in a way that helps you understand it the best, thereby allowing you to achieve the best results possible. All the *Tools* listed are examples. You may use all of them; you may use none of them. Only you can determine what your blueprint calls for. While multiple *Tools* are needed for the job, one strong *Tool* can get any project off the ground.

As you continue through your building process, you will begin to discover *Tools* along the way. They will be handed down to you in the form of advice. You will discover them in your travels as you will now be reading better headspace books and watching less mind-numbing TV. Some you may develop on your own in response to a trouble spot you try to build or repair. For this is how all great *Tools* are developed: in response to need.

If you have a *Tool* that is already working for you and it's not listed above, use it. There is no need to reinvent the wheel. While I believe most of you will start by using the *Tools* I have laid out for you in this book, it is my hope that as you move along through the process, you will have discovered others while developing many of your own. Who knows, if the process grabs you like it did me, maybe you will write a book with your own personal twist, developed out of what you have unveiled from this book and others.

110. It's not what happens to you, it's what you do with what happens to you.

I deliberately left this *Tool* for last. This *Tools* is the sledge hammer of the box because it holds so much power and should be a constant affirmation for life. We discussed earlier that the road to success is always under construction. That to be a hammer you must be constantly willing to build. That you must always understand that things happen — and what you are measured most by is your ability to make the most out of what happens. If you know anything about poker, the best players can make a winning hand out of a losing one. You can never win by folding your cards.

Life is 10 percent what happens to you and 90 percent how you react.

— Charles Swindoll

Ultimately you choose. You make decisions every day that affect your life. You are in control of where you go, and you are in control of how you react to situations that occur along the way. Take control of your life by believing that you are the foreman for everything that happens on the worksite for your life. You determine what the foundation will look like. You are responsible for the timeframes in which things should be built. You are the one who separates what needs to be done now and what can be worked on later. And you determine what *Tools* you are going to use to best build the job, knowing the whole time that the plans will be continuously changing because of a myriad of factors in and out of your control. All the while feeling comfort in understanding that it's not what happens to you, it's what you do with what happens to you. Understanding that you have the ability to make plans to react to the challenges that arise day to day and can set goals to set your efforts in the right direction. Lastly and most importantly, you have chosen to be a hammer in life and you are building the way a hammer should.

Chapter 5:
Custom Homes or
Tract Housing

"Life is what we make it, always has been, always will be."
— Grandma Moses

You now have all the parts of the system. Now you are ready to become a hammer and start to build your life. You have all the things needed to help you build; but you have another decision to make. The question you need to ask yourself is, "Do I want a custom built home or should I simply settle for tract housing?" Simply put, "Do I want something unique or do I want something everyone else has?" Building a custom life is harder. It means coming up with plans that are specific to what you want in life. When you build a custom life, you build something different from all the other lives on the block. Customizing your life comes at a cost; the challenges encountered along the way will require solutions that may take an extra effort to identify. With building a custom life come greater risk — and we already know with greater risk come greater reward. The reward in building something custom is that it was done meeting all the standards that you demand. When people see something custom, they will often stand in awe at what was built.

Building what others have is still building. It requires many of the same efforts as someone who builds a custom life. I am not here to tell you that there is anything wrong with following another's example. If you build your first home, it would be a smart idea to use an example. I feel it's important that you build what you want — and not what you think you should. When building the life you hope for, it is OK to emulate lives that you deem successful. In fact, in *Tool 108* it asks you to find someone you would like to be like. I guess what I am trying to say is: "Don't build what you think others would want you to build."

In an effort to make you feel confident in working on your first worksite, the next few pages provide some case studies that will give you examples of how people from different backgrounds have applied the system in this book to deal with their own situations. I have kept them generic and somewhat cliché to make it simple to see how the blueprint can be applied. The cases will detail their situations, their blueprints, and why they chose the selections for the sections.

CASE STUDY #1

HISTORY: Chad is a 20-year-old college student who is just starting his junior year of college. He ended up at his college of choice because he received a water polo scholarship. Now in his third year of school he finds challenges in his personal life, scholastics and effort needed to compete at the college level. In high school things were easy for Chad. He was the best player on his team and the school work was structured and allowed for little freedom. Now he is competing with other great players and his education requires him to take more responsibility with regard to attendance and study time. Now that he is in college, he has found that there are many more distractions. He has made many new friends and often feels guilty that he neglects old friends. He has become caught up in "the college experience," which causes him to miss workouts and eat foods that he normally would have avoided. He finds himself staying out late on nights that he never has before. This has begun to affect making it to class and his workouts. Chad has found himself in unfamiliar territory. He has started to find class hard and is pretty sure it's because he is now missing some of them. For the first time in his life he feels like he may lose his spot on the water polo team, and he thinks his diet may be causing him to lose his edge.

DISCUSSION: Chad has constructed a mission statement to remind him of two things, what an athlete does and to keep him focused on who he was and still wants to be. His long-term goals mainly focus on the college side of his life, for that is where his main focus is right now, but he did throw in skydiving as something he would like to do in his lifetime. His SELF goals are committed to three areas of need: athletics, school and friends/family. His affirmation confirms this since one of his overall goals is to improve these areas that have faltered over the past two years. His NUTRITION and EXERCISE goals are specified to the demands of his sport. Looking at the *Tools* he has chosen, four of them relate to all his goals but most specially his athletic demands. One he has chosen to deal with his nutritional needs and one to help him remember to keep in touch with friends and family and in doing so, they helped remind him of how he used to be. That is what he's striving for. He wants to restore the habits and attitudes that once made him great.

Mission Statement

I am an elite intercollegiate athlete. An elite athlete commits himself to a regimen of diet and exercise to assist him to excel at his sport. As a student, I will attend class, do all readings and turn in all assignments on time. I will avoid distractions and remember where I came from.

1 2 3 4 5 6 7 8 9 10 11 12 13 14 15 16 17 18 19 20 21

I. *3.5 GPA*

II. *Double major*

III. *Skydive*

IV. *Become a national champion*

V. *Graduate in four years*

VI. *Pay off student loans early*

Self:

- *Go to every class*
- *Keep in touch with family and friends*
- *Make water polo first team*
- *Limit Internet surfing time*

Affirmation:

"I will improve myself in all areas of life."

Nutrition:

- *No fast food*
- *6 small meals per day*
- *Protein powder*

Exercise:

- *Make all training sessions*
- *20 minutes of stretching per day*

Tools:

1. *You don't want it bad enough.*

2. *Eat with your head 1-6; eat with your heart day 7.*

3. *Ultimately you choose.*

4. *The will to win is nothing compared to the will to prepare to win.*

5. *Never settle for anything less than you are capable of achieving.*

6. *Keep in touch.*

X _____

CASE STUDY #2

HISTORY: Lisa is a 29-year-old single mother of one daughter. She is presently employed as an administrative assistant. Lisa found herself in a bit of a rut. She put on some weight over the past few years and has been unable to commit to a workout plan. She feels unhappy at work because she feels stuck and treats it like a job and not a career. She believes she could advance in her job with some more training or her graduate degree but believes there isn't enough time. She has become more negative lately in her personal life too. She started to believe that there are no "good" guys left and sometimes finds herself mad for no reason. She would like to put away money for her daughter's college fund and her own retirement but can't seem to find a way. She just feels lost.

DISCUSSION: Even before Lisa started her blueprint, she began to accept that her present situation was largely due to the mentality she had adopted, and from then on she proclaimed to not play the role of the victim. She would start to take responsibility for her life and understand that she may make some mistakes along the way, but she just won't make them twice. Her mission statement serves as something she needs to hear every day, meaning since there is no one in her life to say it, she has to remind herself. And that's fine because it fits in well with her new attitude. It has been a long time since she really dreamed or even had time to dream. So her long-term goals have more "down-the-road" dreams than most. In her SANE section her listed goals are very precise and simple. This is her first attempt at anything like this and she needs to set herself up for some early wins. Her goals will help her to start saving money, start on that graduate degree, get her headspace right, and start to promote better health. She also has some nice overlap. By limiting mochas and sodas, she will save $30 to $40 a week and cut out some meaningless calories. She also has done a smart thing in the EXERCISE area. She is going to start morning workouts that will help her not have to choose between daughter or workout time. Softball will take her back to making exercise fun and maybe even meeting someone since it is coed. Finally, her AFFIRMATION and *Tools* accomplish the need to change her mind set for now and in the future. She never thought of her brain as a computer and now she is the programmer.

Mission Statement

I believe that I can have the power to create any life that I want for myself. I am in control of my health and appearance, and I will do my best to enhance them. I will set an example that my daughter can be proud of. There is no ceiling to my employment. I refuse to settle for less than the best.

1 2 3 4 5 6 7 8 9 10 11 12 13 14 15 16 17 18 19 20 21

I. *Soul mate*

II. *Promotion*

III. *Graduate degree*

IV. *Open a boutique*

V. *Go on game show*

VI. *Take an RV trip around the U.S.*

Self:

- *Save $50 a paycheck*
- *Start one night class*
- *30 minute alone time*
- *Read and listen to motivational books and CDs*

Affirmation:

"How I think determines how I act."

Nutrition:

- *No soda*
- *No mochas*
- *No late-night meals*
- *Eat breakfast*

Exercise:

- *A.M. workouts*
- *Start coed softball*

Tools:

1. *Be grateful for the things you have and give thanks.*

2. *Connect the rings.*

3. *It takes an hour to burn 500 calories; it takes seconds to eat 500 calories.*

4. *Choose the latte or a million dollars.*

5. *Rich people believe, "I create my life." Poor people believe, "Life happens to me."*

6. *I am not alone.*

X _____

CASE STUDY #3

HISTORY: Jan is a 45-year-old saleswoman, has two kids in high school and has been married for 20 years. She sells advertising for a local radio station and finds it harder to sell spots on her station than it was in the past. She is not sure what has changed but believes it is a combination of the industry and something she is doing or not doing. She used to love radio and got great pleasure out of seeing the results her clients received. She would like to get that feeling back and maybe push for the sales manager position that is opening. Family life is pretty good, but she felt that her family is not as close as they used to be. Things have become routine with everyone's schedules, and they don't spend as much time together on the weekends and they never have family dinner anymore. Her kids will soon be going off to college, and she would like to fix this before they go. Her diet isn't bad but varies based on her schedule, and her workouts have become boring and routine.

DISCUSSION: Jan has two specific areas that are the most important to her right now — her family and career. She is not having problems with either but would like a plan to improve things. She is going to go back to doing the things that worked for her early on in business. In sales, there are things that need to be done, and she has stopped doing them. She is going to go back to doing chamber events and business mixers. She's going to revisit old clients and service them like she has in the past. She has to do two things. First, just work a tad harder, *211 vs. 212,* and second, work a bit smarter, sharpening her axe. Also, she needs to review her wins each week to remind her of the great job she does as a mother, wife and saleswoman. She has come up with a plan to get the family back together. She now knows it won't happen unless she makes it happen. To ensure she doesn't fall out of exercising, she's going to find something new and exciting. She wants a more stable and simple diet. Her blueprint helps her get out of habits that aren't fostering growth, and she knows the best cure for a sluggish mind is to disturb its routine. Lastly, she has some nice long-term goals with regard to work but has scattered in some great ones as she draws closer to her retirement. She is a nice example of someone not in crisis mode, just repair mode. And now she has a repair plan.

Mission Statement

I take great pride in my family and find strength in what we have grown to become. I will make an effort for more family time and events. I am a great saleswoman and will do the little things that made me great. I will treat my body more like a temple, and I will discover new workouts and make nutrition paramount.

1 2 3 4 5 6 7 8 9 10 11 12 13 14 15 16 17 18 19 20 21

I. *Become sales manager*

II. *Become top in sales*

III. *Learn a new language*

IV. *Go on safari*

V. *Write*

VI. *Run for office*

Self:

- *Date night with husband*
- *Set a family dinner time*
- *Family event once a week*
- *Start to re-attend business mixers*
- *Visit with old clients*

Affirmation:

"I judge each day not by the harvest, but the seeds I plant."

Nutrition:

- *Three meals a day, don't skip*
- *Find a meal plan to meet health and exercise goals and my random schedule*

Exercise:

- *Try three new workouts*
- *A.M. workouts*

Tools:

1. *211 vs. 212*

2. *The best cure for a sluggish mind is to disturb its routine.*

3. *Form a Master Mind Group.*

4. *You have to be there mentally before you are physically.*

5. *Review the wins you have each week.*

6. *Sharpen your axe.*

X _____

CASE STUDY #4

HISTORY: Don is 62-years-old and has just retired from his job of over 30 years. He is married and his wife works part time. He has three children who are all out of school and employed. He also has 10 grandchildren. All of his children are out of town but they do live in the same state. Don has a few challenges that have popped up in his life. First, he's never been retired and has no idea what to do. He wants to travel, but has been to many places and feels that there aren't too many places he still needs to see. He never had many hobbies because he worked a lot and most of his focus was on his family. He feels he has never really thought of himself and is feeling a little guilty. He would like to find time to balance family and his own needs and desires. He also would like to live a little and do some things he never has before. He still feels the need to help others and is unwilling to lose that. He also has never done a lot with his health; he has Type II diabetes that his doctor believes can be remedied with diet and exercise. This is also a place he feels lost. He wants to enjoy his retirement and spend time with his grandkids but fears his health risks may interfere with this. Now that he has the time, he is willing to do whatever it takes.

DISCUSSION: Don has constructed a mission statement that will put him in the right frame of mind for the next phase of his life. He has set 200 pounds as his ultimate target weight, but you will notice in his SANE section, he has set 260 pounds as a goal for the next 21 days. He has entered seeing his grandchildren and finding a hobby as something he wants to start right away. He understands that he has little knowledge in the field of nutrition and exercise so he has decided to get experts in these fields. He has also used the *Tool, Get a coach,* to make sure that this goal becomes reality. Don is an example of where I believe the *Tools* are extremely important. This is very new for him and these will help. The *"Why Not Club"* is great for him because it will allow him to get out of his comfort zone. In doing so, he will be more likely to find a hobby and in turn work a little more on himself. *Finding an alternative* will expose him to some viewpoints of health he has never experienced before and he needs it! Also, Don needs to have fun being retired and using the *Tool* of *not acting his age* will let him relax a bit and not worry so much about what others will think. He has worried about others his entire life.

Mission Statement

As I enter a new phase in my life, I will not fear the changes that are to come. I will use this fresh start to concentrate more on myself, my heart and my headspace — these areas must come first because as I improve, I will be better for those around me. I am not afraid.

1 2 3 4 5 6 7 8 9 10 11 12 13 14 15 16 17 18 19 20 21

I. *Lose Type II Diabetes* **II.** *Upgrade house* **III.** *Whole family trip*

IV. *200 Pounds* **V.** *Learn to scuba dive* **VI.** *Rebuild an old car*

Self:

- *Visit grandkids every week*
- *260 pounds*
- *Find a charity to work at two days a week*

Affirmation:

"I let go of old ideas so new ones can enter."

Nutrition:

- *No fast food*
- *Take vitamins*
- *No dessert or candy*
- *Cut down on carbs*
- *Nutritionist*

Exercise:

- *Start with a trainer*

Tools:

1. *Join the "Why Not" Club.*

2. *Become more selfish.*

3. *Get a coach, trainer and nutritionist.*

4. *Accept change as a part of life, don't fight it.*

5. *Stop acting your age.*

6. *Find your alternative.*

X _____

Chapter 6:
Sorry, but This Book is Not the Answer

"Some questions are more important than answers."
— Nancy Willard

Wow! Not a great way to end a book on building a successful life, or is it? What I'm trying to say is that there is no "right" answer for building a successful life. For example, there is not one building that is perfect for every company or one home perfect for every person. Even if you do find the right fit — whether in buildings or life — you may find things change and you need to switch directions. The definition of an answer is the end to any question. So this book can't be the answer because there is no end to the growth process. I admit I'm *playing* with you a bit to make a point.

Just remember, the road to success is always under construction. You're never going to get to a point and say "Ta da." *Be the Hammer Not the Nail* isn't just about building a successful happy life nor is it solely a roadmap to get you from point A to point B. *Be the Hammer Not the Nail* helps you construct the blueprint for your life to develop a structure and framework, and then *maintain* it. You will always need to perform maintenance as any neglect will show. An unkept "building" looks messy and unwelcoming. You know by now exactly how much work needs to be performed on your life. This might be the first real effort you have made toward building that life.

There are no magic bullets in life. Over time we have been conditioned to find some sort of pill or one trick that will make our lives easier. You will work hard to have a successful life — and in the end it will be worth it. It is always more satisfying to achieve something you have worked for than having it given to you. Please understand, no book, person or pill will solve your problems. No book can offer all the solutions. No diet or exercise program is always the "right" one. We have been conditioned to look outside of ourselves for everything that is wrong and how to make everything right. What I know to be most true — look within and focus on yourself and things on the outside will begin to improve. If you look to the outside versus the inside it can lead to blame, excuses or copouts. Accept that your outside life reflects your inner self — and when you understand life works this way you have taken the biggest step toward building the life you expect for yourself. Let me repeat, *the circumstances in your life are a total reflection of you*. When you accept this, there are no limits to your personal growth.

If anything I am saying is untrue, then how do you explain it? How do the miracle stories exist of those who rise out of the worst circumstances and manage to step up and succeed? The endless literature of those who rise above the staunchest set of circumstance and adversity only strengthens the proof that there is a way and a common set of characteristics, strategies and attitudes that facilitate these awesome success stories. If one was to simply chalk it up to luck then, if true, these stories of incredible achievement would have to be spread evenly and randomly amongst all of us. The unequivocal truth that I have learned in my search is that we do make our own reality. If you don't believe me, look at all the people you know who fail and screw up their lives yet have it all — money, education, opportunities and connections. When these people fail, they are the most tragic of stories.

Analyze the two scenarios. There are so many who succeed that shouldn't and there are so many more who should succeed that do not. Tell me if you have a better explanation as to why this happens. It illustrates just how someone can rise above their immediate circumstances if they have the right blueprint for success. To further my point, even when all the circumstances are available to foster one's success, if you do not have the right blueprint, instructions and Tools, nothing else really matters.

Do you decide to buy into the lie? Do you believe your life is simply based on chance? Random chance, you believe in that? If you do, don't believe it. There are too many things in my life that have happened that cannot be explained by chance. If you believed in chance, hopefully after reading *Be the Hammer Not the Nail* you now have new eyes to see how that just isn't possible.

Think about things that have occurred in your own life. If life is only about chance and luck, why work at anything at all? If random chance is true, anything you have worked for and achieved means nothing. It couldn't, because with chance you didn't have anything to do with advancing the outcome. Herein lies a major principle of this book. By using the principles laid out for you in *Be the Hammer Not the Nail,* you drastically improve your probability for success, blowing the random chance camp right out of the water. Decide to buy into the truth that you are in control, you are in the driver's seat, and when you do, you will be able to let go of blame, excuses and self sabotage.

The premises presented in this book may be a lot for you to handle. You may feel that this is too much all at one time. You also may just think this is all a bunch of psycho babble. These are very fair ways for you to be feeling; but let me ask you one question. Is what you have been doing working? If the answer is no, then what have you got to lose by building something you can be proud of? If the answer is kind of, then chances are you are doing some reading, writing and goal setting. Good for you, now let's take it to the next level. If the answer is yes, then that is awesome; you know that another resource for your arsenal is just what you need to keep on reaching the levels you aspire to hit.

One thing that I have accepted is that life is hard. Life is full of highs and lows, wins and losses, and most importantly challenges. Regardless of how we got here, where we are in our lives or where we are going, life is simply a game. You are playing that game whether you like it or not. The game has rules and when you know these rules, you have to come up with a game plan. When you look at life in this way, it gives you the ultimate power to develop your strategy on how you plan to win the game. Constructing the game plan is the hard part if you don't know how. Hopefully you now feel prepared to attack this crucial step to succeeding at the game of life. The best coaches in the world put together game plans their whole lives. Sometimes they win and sometimes they lose. Those who win the most look at those plans after every win and loss and then refine and apply what they learned for the next go around. This is the definition of how to build a life; your life.

I know for a fact we are primed for success. Why? Because we all want something better. It is in our nature to survive and succeed at life. If we can agree on this basic premise, then we must identify what differs between those who succeed and those who don't. Let me be quite clear we are not talking about failure; failure is a major component of success. Our greatest failure is not seeing failure as a part of success. Do not fear the possibility of failure because when you try to run through a door and you hit a wall, the only shortcoming is to keep running into that wall. If I told you there were 10 doors with a million dollars behind one of them and that you could keep opening doors until you found it, what would you do? Well, the answer is obvious when you know you just have to keep opening doors until you find the money. The problem is that most of us stop after only a few doors. We don't realize that each failure leads us closer to that million-dollar door if you keep fighting for it. Even when you know you have the 10th door with all the cash, it may have many locks and even still be quite sticky. If you want the big prize, you have to keep working hard even when you have the right one. Even with all the keys, you may have to break down that door to get what you want.

Let me leave you with a story that I had previously read but forgotten. I rediscovered it the day I wrote this chapter as I was reading my journal during lunch.

The Carpenter

An elderly carpenter was ready to retire. He told his employer-contractor of his plans to leave the house-building business and live a more leisurely life with his wife and enjoy his extended family. He would miss the paycheck, but he needed to retire; they could get by.

The contractor was sorry to see his good worker go and asked if he would build just one more house as a personal favor. The carpenter said yes, but in time it was easy to see that his heart was not in his work. He resorted to shoddy workmanship and used inferior materials. It was an unfortunate way to end his career.

When the carpenter finished his work and the builder came to inspect the house, the contractor handed the front-door key to the carpenter, "This is your house," he said, "my gift to you."

What a shock! What a shame! If he had only known he was building his own house, he would have done it all so differently. Now he had to live in a home that he had built none too well.

So it is with us. We build our lives in a distracted way, reacting rather than acting, willing to put forth less than our best. At important points we do not give the job our best effort. Then with a shock, we look at the situation we have created and find that we are now living in the house we have built. If we had realized that, we would have done it differently.

Think of yourself as the carpenter. Think about your house. Each day you hammer a nail, place a board, or erect a wall. Build it wisely.

It is the only life you will ever build. Even if you live for only one more day, that day deserves to be lived graciously and with dignity.

The plaque on the wall says, "Life is a do-it-yourself project." Who could say it more clearly? Your life today is the result of your attitudes and choices in the past. Your life tomorrow will be the result of the attitudes and choices you make today.

— Author Unknown

About the Author

Dr. Lance A. Casazza wrote *Be the Hammer Not the Nail* to help millions of people searching for a practical and useful self-help book to improve their lives. After spending several years struggling in his private practice, Dr. Casazza began a personal odyssey to discover what successful people did to realize their dreams. This book is the result of his research, dedication and commitment to find answers and help others build the lives of their dreams.

Dr. Casazza is a graduate of the Palmer College of Chiropractic West, New College of California, and earned a Bachelor's Degree in Exercise Science from the University of California, Davis. He has published several articles including: *Sacramento News & Review,* "Ask Dr. Lance"; and *Dynamic Chiropractic,* "The Association of Smoking and Low Back Pain."

He currently lives in Sacramento, California and successfully runs his private practice, Casazza Chiropractic (http://www.sacramentochiropractic.com).